Frederick Demerchant

Miracle
From First Pit Pond
By
Frederick Demerchant

Frederick Demerchant

Miracle From First Pit Pond
Frederick Demerchant

Published By Parables
November, 2021

All Rights Reserved. No part of this book may be reproduced or utilized in any form or by any means, electronic or mechanical, including photocopying, recording, or by any information storage and retrieval system, without permission in writing from the author.

    Printed in the United States of America

Readers should be aware that Internet Web sites offered as citations and/or sources for further information may have been changed or disappeared between the time this was written and the time it is read.

Miracle From First Pit Pond
By
Frederick Demerchant

Frederick Demerchant

Miracle From First Pit Pond

Chapter 1: Gathering David for Chore-Time

Sarah Gallagher was as tough as she was beautiful. She was the miracle, the miracle that held the Gallagher family together. Well at least before the miracle from First Pit Pond.

"Sarah have you seen your brother David?" Michael Gallagher asks as he's walking into the barn with a bundle of hay in each hand.

"No," says Sarah as she's sweeping up a stall.

This farm is in enough trouble. Trouble let alone, David not here to do his chores.

"Hey, dad." A loud voice cries.

"Yes, Joseph," says Michael.

"Did anyone drive up to First Pit Pond and check there? He's probably up there."

"This close to dark?" his dad asks.

Sarah giggles and says "Him and those Gardner boys would never go home if they could rig up lights up there."

Joseph breaks out laughing. "One night about 8 pm Mrs. Cairns called and said she couldn't find her son and wanted to know if he was with David. Before I had the chance to answer Mrs. Gardner was pulling into the yard looking for her two boys. That's when Sarah suggested we go to First Pit Pond. So Mrs. Gardner, Sarah, and I drove up. There was Darrell Cairns, Marty and LeRoy Gardner. Peter Eales, Brandon Copp, and David all on the pond playing hockey by bonfire light!!!! They must have had a bonfire burning eight feet high!"

"A bonfire?" Asks Micael, "How did they do that?

"Because LeRoy Gardner, shall we say, borrowed his grandpa's chainsaw, and gas jug, and cut a lot of dead treetops, five feet up off the stump."

Saraha laughs and says, "the logging company that owns the land wouldn't be laughing. They must have cut down a cord and a half of wood to build and maintain a bonfire that big."

Joseph and Michael giggle as well! "Well that's quite a tale," says Michael. "It doesn't pay the mortgage on this farm."

"We better get up there," Joseph says.

"Dad, I have all the eggs gathered, what would you like me to do now?" A little 9-year-old voice says.

"Run them into your mother Kevin. Take a bath and say your prayers. I'll be in to tuck you in soon."

"He is such a great help dad," replies Sarah as Kevin shuts the barn door.

"Yes, you are all wonderful and great!" Replies Michael. A tear falls from Michael's eye as he says that. Sarah runs over to her father immediately, grabs him by the shoulders, "dad what's wrong?"

"Ohhhh Sarah" her dad says. "I just hope I can save this farm for him, you, Joseph, and David.

Joseph looks at his dad and smiles "Not David dad, remember he's going straight to the NHL outta high school."

Sarah laughs, "I think you should too, Joseph. That or wrestling, what with your big broad shoulders." They all hug as a family and laugh!!

"Oh Kids, I thank God for you all every day!" says Michael. "Your wonderful mother too!!!"

Sarah giggles "dad are you sure? She's the one who always encourages David of his NHL dreams.

Her dad laughs "Yes Saraha even her too!" Donna June Gallagher always encouraged all her children! She was a great mom and a great wife!! "We better drive up to First Pit Pond and get David," replies Michael. "These water troughs aren't gonna fill themselves."

"Let's go," Joseph smiles and says. "Let's go, let's go, let's go!!!!"

****

Darrell says, "I gotta be home before dark."

"So do I," says Stephen Theriault. "And it's a 15-minute snowmobile ride to get home to McAdam."

"Come on guys, just 5 more minutes!!!"

"Man, I hope you do make the NHL," says Darrell. "There cannot be anyone on the planet with a love for hockey greater than you have!!"

"Okay guys," says Stephen, "just 5 more minutes but only if David agrees to tell us the secret of his shot. He gets the puck into my net every time. I can't stop it."

"Ok guys listen, I'm 16 years old."

"Ya, and so?" asks LeRoy.

"I have been lugging water into my dad's cows in the barn for like 12 years. My earliest memories are watching Toronto Maple Leafs play Boston Bruins on televisions and lugging water to those cows!"

"What does that have to do with your shot?" asks Stephen.

"Let me explain. Every time I'd take my bucket and dump it in quickly, I'd always get a little splash back. Now April to November it's not so bad when that happens. But in January, February and well into March, it's cold enough without cold water splashing on you. So I learned to gently dump my bucket and swirl it at the same time."

"Yea, yea I notice you keep tapping the puck where the horizontal meets the vertical part of your hockey stick," says LeRoy.

"Yes" answers David. "This causes the puck to keep spinning or swirling if you will. Then one good smack with my 145 lbs of body power and BAM, a goal every time!"

"By the way, no one gets into the NHL at 145 lbs," says Stephen.

"I don't know, Bobby and Brett Hall weren't massive and they did alright," says LeRoy.

"So you learned all that from watering cows?" asks Darrell.

"No, not really," says David.

"Well how else did you learn?" asks LeRoy.

"By watching science fiction movies," says David.

"Science fiction movies?" asks Darrell.

"Yes. When a spaceship leaves at a high rate of speed it is always spinning around and around," says David.

"Don't tell me you believe in all that too," says Darrell.

"Believe in what?" asks David.

"Spaceships and aliens," says Darrell.

"Guys I have more interest than just hockey," says David. They all laugh as David quickly grabs the puck and goes around the pond. Darrell and Stephen get back in their nets and it's the same as it was many afternoons in St. Croix, New Brunswick.

Just as soon as it started, Micael, Sarah, and Joseph pulled up to the side of the road. Joseph gets out of the car and hollers "Ok Bobby Clark lets go!!!"

"Hey Joseph don't you mean Bobby Orr?" Sarah laughs. David skates to the end of the pond as his sister and dad are standing there. Big brother Joseph smiles and waves from the car.

"Hi Mr. Gallagher."

"Hi Saraha," says LeRoy. "Hi" they answer back.

"Now dad and Sarah, I am very flattered that you guys would refer to me as Bobby Clark or Bobby Orr but there are important things you're forgetting."

"What's that?" asks Sarah.

"Bobby Orr played for the Boston Bruins, and Bobby Clark played for the Philadelphia Flyers, but I'm gonna play for my favorite team in the world, the Toronto Maples Leafs!!

"Ok Lanny MacDonald. Let's go," shouts Joseph from the car.

"He played for Calgary," shouts Darrell. They all laugh.

"And the second thing is this," says David.

"What's that son?" his father asks as David unlaces his skates, sitting on the frozen snowbank.

"You will see Gallagher on the back of a Maple Leafs jersey one day."

"Mine!!!! Ok let's go guy Lafleur" says Sarah.

"No it's Gallagher, not Lafleur, but he's a pretty good guy though even though he does play for the Habs."

Everybody breaks out laughing hard.

"Guys get your skates off. I'll run David to the barn to do his chores and I'll be back to give you guys a ride home."

"I have my snowmobile, Mr. Gallagher," says Stephen.

"Ok, no problem. You be careful driving into McAdam."

"I will sir," says Stephen.

Sarah, Micheal, Joseph, and David hop in the car and drive home to the farm. Yes, things weren't all bad in St. Croix, New

Brunswick, but some challenging things were laying ahead. They were about to learn what love of a family was for.

Frederick Demerchant

Chapter 2: First of the Month in more Ways than One

Yes, the Gallagher family was made up of six souls. All very different but all similar in ways too. The mother, Donna was the oldest, she was 43. A kind woman with an amazing smile and a love for the simple things in life. Donna loved her children, and singing along with the gospel radio station and baking homemade pies. Her husband Micaeal was 40. He was a fairly tall man around 6 ft and 200 lbs. His hair was once raven black but with age and circumstance of life, it was starting to get quite gray on the sides. Although he wore the salt and pepper look well. Michael had a lot of wisdom that came with that hair, but in all honesty a little worry as well. Michael bought and started the farm when he was only 24 years old. A wife and a baby soon afterward puts a lot of pressure on a man in his early 20's. It was all good. Michael had a great faith, a great love for God, and a great love for his family. But with the rising cost of everything from feed to tractor parts, and five mouths to feed plus his own, life wasn't always easy in Southwest New Brunswick. But Michael loved his family and loved his farm which they all worked so hard at, and they all loved so much. Well all but David. He didn't really mind the farm but his heart was in hockey. Joseph Gallagher was just barely 18, but to look at him you would never know it. He had his dad's height beaten by an inch and his weight by 19 lbs. Yes Joseph was 6'1'' tall and 219 lbs. I guess with four farm fresh eggs every morning and a bowl of Red River Cereal and a love for farming like his dad and hours and hours of hard work oh and let's not forget good genes, 6'1'', 219 lbs is what you get. Joseph had curly chestnut hair like his mom and he had her disposition as well. A love for the simple quaint things in life.

David was 17 now. His facial features were his father through and through. Raven dark hair and green sparkling eyes and a strong jawline. His height was 5'10'' and he weighed 147 lbs wringing soaking wet. Sarah Elizabeth Gallagher well she was a lot of things, but mostly the glue that held the Gallaghers together. 14 years of age, but wise beyond her years. She also had her mom's beautiful chestnut curly hair that fell three to four inches below her shoulders and her dad's sparkling green eyes, fair skin and was turning into a beautiful young lady. Oh, she was feisty though. One time in grade 7 she was doing her morning chores and she was running a little late and didn't have time to take her gum rubbers off and put her school shoes on, so she wore them to school. Two girls in grade 9 made fun of Sarah. One said "nice shoes farm girl!!"
Sarah ran up and grabbed her by the shoulders and gave her that boot right in the butt. The other girl got so scared she ran away. But Sarah, like her brother David, has some athletic ability. She took the boot off and threw it at her and hit her in the head with it. Well after a meeting with principal Kelly, a one day suspension and staying after school till 4:30pm for two nights, life returned back to normal for Sarah. But let me tell you what, nobody said a word to Sarah again. Sarah was a great student. Second in her class and everybody loved Sarah's no nonsense attitude. At just 5'2'' and 110 lbs, Sarah Gallagher took no guff!!! But she had a heart of gold and a love for God and for her family! Every night she used to pray "Jesus let me be just like you in every aspect of my life, but let me fight like the devil if I have to". Kevin Gallagher was 9 years old. A shy kid, very quiet. But like all the Gallaghers, he shared a great work ethic and enjoyed farm life. He had blue eyes and very dark hair like his dad.

One day when the kids were off at school Donna shouted out the front door to her husband Michael. "Michael."
"Yes sweetheart," he said.
"Come on in for some coffee and homemade apple pie and I'll get all the financial reports like you asked."
"Ok, dear. I'll be right in," he replied.

Miracle From First Pit Pond

Now Micaeal loved the idea of Donna's homemade apple pie and a hot fresh cup of coffee on this frosty winters day, but he didn't like the sound of going over the financial reports. Now feed for cows and chickens, rising taxes and upkeep on old barns plus new construction of the big barn, three and a half years of rising cost of potato seed, well it was almost enough to concern any
savvy financial person! But put four growing children's mouths to feed plus Donna June's and his own, well to say the least it was challenging for Michael.
"Hi hunny," Donna warmly said as Michael came in. "Pie is on the table, my love, and I'll pour you a fresh hot cup."
"Ok," Michael kindly muttered.
"Sweetheart, what's wrong?" Donna June asked.
"Well I just dread big time going over these financial reports."
"We will make it, we always do," replies Donna June.
"Yes, but feed is going up and even when we buy it over in Maine, what with our dollar being down right now and duty on top of it, we don't save much."
"Yes hunny, but don't forget 15% of all duty we pay is reimbursed back to us under the New Brunswick Farm substitute act. So that helps come tax time in the spring. Also a lot of people in the community have requisitions about buying pork. Maybe we should look into purchasing three or four pigs."
"I thought of that dear, but pig feed is rising as well," replied Michael.
"Well it's the first of the month in more ways than one next week," said Michael.
"What do you mean dear?" asked Donna
"Well our $511 payment on the farm is due, and Sarah's $25 trip fund is due. It's the first of four payments back to back. February, March, April, May. Then they leave for their four day four night class trip to Prince Edward Island."
"I've never been there," said Donna June.
"Maybe one day when the kids are all grown you and I can go over sometime. I was there once with my mom and uncle John when I was a boy, it was beautiful," replied Michael.

"I am glad you enjoyed it hunny," replied Donne June. But do you know what Donna said as Michael ate his last piece of homemade apple pie, as he winked and smiled at his wife.
"Sarah is a great girl!!! A lot like her daddy," Donna June said.
"She will understand if we can't afford it."
"No way," said Michael after chugging a big swig of coffee. "She works almost as many hours on this farm as I do, never complains ever, and is a great student. She deserves this trip and she's gonna have it. And besides, I believe she is the glue that holds this family together."
"Well it's almost the first of February. We owe the farm payment of $511 to the bank and now four straight months of $25 payments on top of it. Maybe I could sell more pies to help, they were a hit at the church Christmas social and at $5.50 and an average overall cost of $3.00 per pie to make, that's an overall profit of $2.50 per pie!!!
"Thank the good Lord I planted that MacIntosh apple tree the day I married you!!" replied Michael. "That has provided a pile of apples for your pies."
"Hey I'll be making peach pies and lemon meranges too!!" replies Donne June.
"What am I supposed to do, plant a lemon tree and peach tree this spring as well?" asks Michael.
Donna June takes his hand and smiles and says, "no I don't think they will stand up to our New Brunswick climate." They both laugh. Donna rises out of her chair and hugs him. "I love you Michael Oliver Gallagher!!"
"Hand me the good book please sweetheart!!!" They hold hands and Micheal reads one of their, and a lot of peoples, favorite passages from the Bible. The 23rd Psalm. *The Lord is my shepherd, I shall not want. He maketh me to lie down in green pastures, he leadeth me beside the still waters. He restoreth my soul. He leadeth me in the paths of righteousness for his name's sake. Yea though I walk through the valley of the shadow of death, I will fear no evil for thou art with me, thy rod and thy staff they comfort me. Thou preparest a table before me in the presence of mine enemies. Thou anointest my head with oil. My cup runneth*

over. Surely goodness and mercy shall follow me all the days of my life and I will dwell in the house of the Lord forever.
"Amen," says Donna.
"Amen," says Michael.
"So that's the answer," replied Donna June. Selling pies and the farm revenue and the good Lord above. Now $25 a month for a class trip for your child, and a farm payment of $511 isn't chump change in any day and age. But in 1986 it was just as challenging!!
"No," says Michael there are more things as well.
"What's that sweetheart?"
"I am going to see Mr. Walker,"
" Mr. Timothy Walker?" asks Donna June.
"Yes that's right," replies Michael. "Mr. Timothy Walker was the general manager of the forestry company based in St. Croix, New Brunswick, Southwest Valley Pulpwood Ltd. He had contractors from as far as Riviere Du Loup, Quebec and everywhere in between logging for him. And perhaps Michael could get a small block to cut to help pay his farm payments. And maybe perhaps not. But all he could do is speak to Mr. Walker and try. As Michael pulled into the office of Southwest Valley Pulpwood Ltd., he was greeted by a nice man who went to his church named Darren who was a foreman for the company. "Good morning Michael, how are you this morning?"
"Good thank you," Michael replied, "and you?"
"Oh, I'd be a fool to complain. God is good," says Darren.
"Yes he is," Michael smiled and replied.
"Have a great day, and see you on Sunday," Darren said as he gets into his company halfton.
As Micheal was just about to the office door, Darren shouted out, "Hey Michael."
Michael turned and looked at Darren sitting in his company halfton. Darren smiled and said "say hello to all of those wonderful kids of yours for me."
"I will," Michael smiled and replied.
Darren smiled and said, "hey, who do you think lives for hockey more and eat and breathes it more? My boy Stephen or your boy David?"
"I don't know," Micheal says, "they both seem to like it a lot."

Darren smiles and says "nothing wrong with that I guess. You and Donna June, come over and visit Rose and I some evening." Michael smiled and said "we will."
"Those boys and hockey," Darren said as he pulled over to the north brook road to go see his cutting operation.

See Darren Theriault was Stephen's dad. David's friend and the boy who loved to play goalie at First Pit Pond. Before Michael reached for the door knob, he paused for a minute to reflect, or maybe you could say God's peace. The peace that passes all understanding swept over him for a moment. But he thought for a moment, how lucky he was. Four great healthy kids. A loving wife of over 18 years and he worked for himself doing what he truly loved; farming. He truly was blessed. He looked up towards Heaven very quickly and smiled and said, "Thank you God for all you have blessed me with!!!!" As he opened the door and walked in a young secretary greeted him with a smile. "Well good morning Michael, how are you doing this morning?"
"Just fine," Michael smiled and said.
"Are you here looking for more sawdust shavings for farm bedding?" she asked.
"No, I'd like to see Mr. Walker if he's available, please."
"Oh, sure!!" she smiled and said. "Just let me go check and see if he's available."
"Thank you," Michael replied.
The young secretary's name was Rhoda. Rhoda walked to Mr. Walker's door and knocked. Mr. Walker looked up from this paperwork and smiled. "Hi Rhoda," Mr. Walker replied.
"Mr. Walker, Michael Gallagher is here, he would like to see you for a few minutes if you're able."
"By all means give me two minutes and send him in please."
"Thank you sir," Rhoda said. "He will see you in two minutes Michael," she replied and sat back at her desk."Fresh coffee is on just around the corner. Feel free to grab one if you like," she smiled and said to Michael.

Miracle From First Pit Pond

"Thanks, I will," Michael replied. As Michael grabbed a styrofoam cup and hit the button for hot fresh coffee, Rhoda asked him a question.

"Hey Michael, those pies your wife makes for the church Christmas socials are delicious!!! Has she ever considered taking orders for those?"

Michael says, as he smiles, "funny you should ask. We just talked about it yesterday. She is taking orders and they're officially for sale!!"

"Oh that's wonderful," Rhoda replied. "Her homemade apple pies are a little piece of Heaven on this earth!"

"Don't I know it," Michael smiles and says.

Both Rhoda and Michael smile and laugh. The intercom buzzes.

"Miss Johnson,"

"Yes Mr. Walker?"

"Please send in Mr. Gallagher now."

"Yes sir. He's ready to see you now Michael."

"Great to see you Rhoda."

"You too, Michael," Rhoda smiles and says.

Michael walks in. At the desk sits a big man, chewing and sucking on his cigar. A big hand comes out to clasp into Michael's.

"Michael, great to see you as always," Mr. Walker smiles and says.

"Thanks, Mr. Walker, you as well," Michael replies.

Timothy Walker flew fighter planes in World War II, and he got a degree in forestry management when he came home from the war. He left at the age of 19 in 1942 but when he got home again in 1945 he looked as though he was 35. I suppose this life will age you enough, but he was only 22 when he went in college and 26 years of age when he obtained his degree. But fighting the Germans over the skies of Europe, and 3am bombing raids, probably helped to make him look older too, when he returned back home. But now, Mr. Walker was the age of 66 and looked good for his age. He started with Southwest Valley Pulpwood in 1973 at the age of 51 and now at 66 he was enjoying his role as general manager. Southwest Valley Pulpwood had brought a lot of prosperity to Southwest, New Brunswick, Canada. And Mr. Walker was the man at the helm.

"How is the farming business, Michael?" Mr. Walker asks as he shakes Michael's hand.

"Well it's a little rough right now," he replies. "How is the logging business?"

"You thinking of selling your farm and becoming a logging contractor?" Asks Mr. Walker.

"Oh, no sir, right now dairy and beef prices are down quite badly, but unfortunately the cost of feed keeps rising. Now I have eggs and chickens as well and the prices of those are good but it's not enough to offset the cost for the other stuff. I am struggling to feed the family, feed the animals and pay the farm mortgage."

"Hmmm…." says Mr. Walker as he takes the cigar out of his mouth and puts it in the ashtray. "Well how many acres is the farm?" asks, Mr. Walker.

"114 acres and as you probably know, because Southwest Valley Pulpwood land butts up against mine. I am actively farming 65 to 67 acres, the rest is swamp and woodland. So what I wanted to ask you was would I be able to stumpage 20 acres of ground from the company? My oldest son, Joseph and I could cut the pulpwood and the extra money would help carry us through until prices got better, which market analysts say should happen come early spring."

"Hmmm…..," says Mr. Walker. "Well Michael, let me ask you this. That swamp of yours, how many acres is it?"

"I would say it's roughly 11 to 12 acres Mr. Walker."

"Ok, is there much cedar down there?"

"Yes that's exactly what's there. I'd say it's 85-90% cedar. It's fairly big cedar as well. I'd say it probably hasn't been cut since pre World War II. When I bought the land off Elmer Scott, he said he's never cut it. Some of the old trails are still accessible in the wintertime."

"Well Michael here is what I am willing to do. If I can put a small dozer on your land and tramp a winter road out through to the main road, and put a small skidder and crew in to selective cut that cedar, I'll pay you $89 per cord roadside. I will take care of the cutting and tamping the winter road."

"Wow, why so much?" Asks Michael.

"Right now the southern USA fence market is red hot. They are paying $205 per cord USA dollars landed to the mill over in Maine. Cedar makes great fence. I figure I'll have around $152 per cord Canadian to cut, load, tamp road and truck it over. That leaves the company about $92 to $93 per cord with the current exchange rate. A good deal for us both, wouldn't you say?"

"Oh, yes sir!!!" Micheal smiles and replies. "Thank you very, very much."

"You're welcome," says Mr. Walker. "I can't do a 20 acre stumpage to you for pulpwood, but I can do a 14 acre. It's a new company rule brought in this fall. Anyone who isn't an active contractor can still cut for us but on a 14 acre lot and only harvest in the wintertime."

"Thanks Mr. Walker, I really appreciate this."

"Hey, I'll put you down on the Conelly road. Varadine contracting is working way in back, so they are plowing the road. It is only three miles down the road from your farm and it's good frozen ground. Will you be stumpaging with your horse or with your tractor?"

"My tractor, Mr. Walker."

"What is pulp paying these days, $65 per cord roadside?"

"No it's down a little, $61 per cord roadside."

"Hey, it's all good," replies Micheal. "I'll take it!!! Thanks very much Mr. Walker."

"You're welcome," Mr. Walker smiled and replied.

As Michael walked out and got into his station wagon, he felt good about his meeting with Mr. Walker. "We just may pull through after all" he thought as he was driving back home. But logging, like farming, is tough, hard work, not for the faint of heart to say the least. But Timothy Walker was as honest as they come. Michael knew his word was golden.

As Michael pulled into the driveway he shut his car off and looked around his farm. Seven jersey cows grazing on hay, Joseph put out before he left for school. Chickens clucking in the barn, and eighteen beef cows just kind of huddled together with breath leaving out of their nostrils, on this cold winter morning. Michael took off his hat and bowed his head."God thank you for my family and my farm. Thank you for your love. I pray this is the answer for everything. In Jesus' name, Amen." Michael walks into the house.

"Donna, Donna June," he calls out.
"Hey sweetheart!!!! How did the meeting go with Mr. Walker?"
"Well he gave us 14 acres on Conelly road to stumpage and he's paying us $89 per cord roadside for cedar from our swamp in back."
"Well how will you cut both?" Asks Donna June.
"Well that's the thing. I don't have to. Mr. Walker is gonna put a crew in to cut and tamp a winter road with the dozer but we still get $89 per cord cause cedar is used for fencing and that southern US fencing market is red hot right now they can't get it quick enough."
"Well that's great news," replies Donna June.
"Oh, and by the way, Rhoda Johnson wants an apple pie made. But for when I don't know, better call her up and ask! I love you Donna June!"
"I love you sweetheart!!" Replies Donna June to Michael.
On that cold winters day, you could have melted an iceberg with the warmth of the love flowing from that old farm house. But the warmth of spring would soon be here. Time to get to work and do some winter logging!!

Chapter 3: And Spring Turns into Summer

"Sweetheart, sweetheart," Donna June calls as she walks into the barn. "Come on in, I got your favorite mid spring pie made. Lemon marangie!"
"Sounds wonderful hunny," replied Michael.
"Yep, and I got a big ole picture of ice tea made to wash it down with on this hot spring mid May day."
"Ok, I'll be right in," replies Micheal."
"Hurry up sweetie, while you were milking, Mr. Walker dropped off the last cheque for the last 12 cords of cedar they cut and hauled last winter. So we will dig out our books and see where we stand."
"Ok," Michael smiled and said. The Gallagher family and farm had survived another winter.
Michael smiled and said "The good Lord took the Gallagher family through another winter!"
"Amen," Donna June smiles and replies!!

Michael walked into the house and a huge slice of lemon meringue pie was on the table with a tall 16oz glass of ice tea packed with ice cubes. Michael walks over to the cupboard where Dona June was reaching up to grab the financial folder. He reaches from behind and places his hand around her chest and pulls her to him with his big strong forearm.

"Hunny thank you for that wonderful lemon maringine pie and ice tea!!!"
The Gallaghers had a strong love for family and a strong love for one another. That was probably what got them through some hard

times in Southwest New Brunswick. As Michael sat and bowed his head, Donna June poured a glass of ice tea.

"Lord, thank you for this beautiful warm spring day. Thank you for my wonderful wife Donna June that you gave me, and thank you for this wonderful lemon merangine pie and ice tea!!!"

Donna June walked across the kitchen floor and whispered in his ear "Amen" and gave him a kiss on his cheek. Michael grabbed his fork and smiled and dove right into that pie like there was no tomorrow. Donna June takes a sip of ice tea and opens the folder.

"Ok, sweetheart. We have June's payment all covered for the farm mortgage, and about $287 towards July's payment."

"That's wonderful hunny!!!!" Replies Michael

"Sarah's trip to Prince Edward Island is paid and we were able to give her $14 for spending money."

"Oh, that's great hunny. I'm so glad," replies Michael.

"Well that cedar price being through the roof helped a lot. Mr. Walker was very, very fair on his scale of the wood as well. Also, sweetheart, beef prices have risen 5% so that will help us a lot too."

Michael pushes himself away from the table. "That pie was great!!! Thank you, sweetie!!! Well I will go collect the eggs and whatever else needs done."

"Maybe if you're good, you can have another piece for dessert with your grill cheese that I'm making for lunch."

"Ok, sounds great! I love you Donna June," Michael says as he walks out the door. He turns and asks "Oh, hunny?"

"Yes, dear?" Donna June replies.

"Was there anything left of the fund from the cedar and pulpwood?" He asks.

"Yes. $53," replies Donna June. "I got that in the emergency fund."

"Okkee dokkee," he replies "Love you," he says. "I can't wait till Sarah

gets home from school to tell her the great news!!! She will be ecstatic!!"

"I hear ya hunny!" Michael shouts as he walks into the barn.

Miracle From First Pit Pond

****

"Yup see Stephen it's all down here. I got forty-nine goals in twenty three games we played on First Pit Pond. You had two shutouts in nineteen games and three game saving saves!!! You see with these kinds of records, we are prime for the NHL."
"Umm….David I know it's your dream, but I mean come on do you really think we will have a shot? I mean we are kids on a pond in our home in Southwest, New Brunswick."
"No, no, no," replies David. "We are kids from First Pit Pond, and I'm telling you when we get to the NHL and break records, there we will be known, loved and remembered as the kids from First Pit Pond!!!
"Mr. Gallagher, excuse me Mr. Gallagher, let me guess, you and Mr. Theriault are discussing hockey!!"
"Well of course it's our future!!!" David smiles and replies.
"Ha, ha, ha," the class laughs.
"Mr. Gallagher maybe it will, maybe it won't but for the next, Mr. Smith pauses and looks at his watch, twenty-one minutes of your future, it should be concentrating on social studies class!!"
"Yes sir, I'm sorry Mr. Smith," replies David
"Mr. Theriault, don't egg him on."
"Me!!!!?" replies Stephen, "He eggs me on!!"
All the kids laugh again.
"Okay class. settle down." Mr. Smith walks back up to the front of the classroom. "Now after Confederation in 1867, his voice fades into the background.
"Pssssst, Stephen, Stephen."
"David, we will talk after class, you're gonna get us in trouble!"
"Well listen, I am gonna make it to the NHL and if I get there first, I'm taking you with me!"
"Ok pal, thanks," whispers Stephen.
David smiles and gives a thumbs up.

David Gallagher was a mischievous young man, but far from a stupid young man. He had great love for this family and great love for his friends! But his greatest love, earthly love, for his greatest love was for his Lord and saviour Jesus Christ, was the game that he and tens of thousands of Canadian boys loved. Hockey!!! Ever since David was a little boy of four years old, all he ever had dreamed about was being a professional national league hockey player!

David had spent countless hours on that pond, but at 145 lbs and 5'10'' tall was the NHL just a pipe dream for David? Then he quickly remembered his mom watching him, swirl his water bucket in the barn many years ago.
"David what are you doing?" she asked.
"I'm swirling the bucket so the water doesn't splash on me and do you know what I think mama?"
"What's that sweetheart?" Donna June replies.
"I think I can perfect a shot from this swirling mechanism technique."
"A hockey shot?" his mom asks.
"Yes a hockey shot," David replies.
"Out of the mouths of babes," his mom smiles and says, "as the good book says."
For David was just a little kid when he said this, maybe seven years old at best.
"Well hunny, I think you can do it. You can do or be anything if you believe it, sweetheart."
"Anything?" asks David.
"Yes hunny, anything," his beautiful mother smiles and replies.
"Well that settles it," says young David, "I am gonna play for the NHL."
"I believe one day you will!" His mom smiles and says. "Now let's go gather some eggs after you are done practicing your swirling technique."
"I love you mom," David smiles and says.
"I love you too sweetheart."

The school bell rings to end the school period.
"Hi David," a kind voice says.
"Oh, hi Marla! How are you?" David asks.

Miracle From First Pit Pond

"Oh I am good thanks. So are you going to youth group tonight?" Marla asks.
"I sure am, how about you Marla?"
"Yup and pastor Ray is having a birthday cake for us afterward because it's Kim's birthday."
"Oh ya, I forgot. How about that!" replies David.
"I never ever forget," says Marla, "because I have it burned in my brain."
"Have it burned in your brain, how?" asks David.
"The three magic Fridays in a row," Marla smiles and replies.
"June 8th is Kim's birthday. June 15th is your birthday and June 22nd is the last day of school!!! So I call them the tree magic Fridays!"
David smiles and says "what happens if they fall on Tuesday next year, will they all be magic Tuesdays?"
Marla gently punches his shoulder and smiles. "You know what I mean!"
"I know, I know," David smiles and says. They both giggle."I'll see you tonight David." Marla smiles and walks down the school hallway. David grabs his bookbag and jean jacket from his locker and thinks to himself how lucky he is to have such good friends and family and a dream!!! A dream of becoming an NHL player. Now that dream may be a hard row to hoe, but David didn't mind. He was a farm kid! Hard rows to hoe were part of his life literally!!! As he walks his way down to the bus, he feels a hand on his shoulder and a familiar friendly voice.
"Well hi big brother, how was your school day?"
"Good thanks and yours?" David replied.
"Great," says Sarah! Now we just gotta get our farm chores done, and then youth group tonight."
"Yea it's gonna be a nice youth group tonight," says David.
"Pastor Ray is bringing a cake, did you know that?" asks David.
"Because it's Kim's birthday," Sarah replies.
"That's right, how did you know that?" David asks Sarah as he gets on the school bus.
"I'm not just another pretty face, big brother. I'm quite knowledgeable, you know."
"I know, I know," David laughs and says.

"I'll be making two cakes to take to next week's youth group," says Sarah "One for your birthday and for Pastor Ray for appreciation to him."
"That's nice Sarah" David says.
"How did you remember next week is my birthday?"
"Two reasons," Sarah says. "Number one, I love you. Number two I'm not just another pretty face. I'm quite smart and knowledgeable!!"
"Yes it would appear so!" says David.
They smile at each other and laugh. "I love you lil sis."
"And I love you big brother."
As the bus pulls into gear and the kids start their journey home. After about fourteen to fifteen stops and about twenty seven to twenty eight kids getting off the bus, the Gallagher kids were all home. As they walk to their farmhouse Sarah asks Joseph "So big brother your big day is almost here! Have you given any thought to university, college or community college?"
As Sarah is asking those things of Joseph, Joseph reaches over, grabs Kevin by his hips and in one foul swoop hurls him into the air and Kevin lands on Joseph's big strong shoulders.
"Whoo Hoo Ha, thanks big brother!!!" Kevin shouts with glee
"Hey, anything for you little brother." Joseph replies. Sarah and David smile at each other.
As these activities are taking place, Donna June is standing by the kitchen window. Michael is right by her side. Michael puts his arm around Donna June and says "we got four great kids!"
"We sure do," Donna June says as the children are walking up the drive.
"I don't know," Joseph replies to Sarah. "I thought about possibly taking welding or mechanics, but I'm not sure."
"Those are both good fields to get into," Sarah says to Joseph.
"But I haven't applied anywhere," says Joseph. "I think I just wanna work on the farm for the summer and fall, and maybe apply in the late fall and early winter for fall classes in 1986.
"Well don't put it off too long," says Sarah.
"Yea big brother," shouts little Kevin. "I'm here to water cows and gather eggs," says little Kevin.

"And I'm here to clean stalls," says Sarah.
"Well I guess you guys got it all sewed up," says Joseph, as they all walk through the door of their country farmhouse.
"Children, your father and I just want you to know we love you very, very much, and we are so happy, blessed and lucky to have you in our lives."
"No mother," says Sarah. " Joseph, Kevin, David and I are the lucky ones! Lucky and blessed to have you as our wonderful kind loving, guiding parents!"
"Amen," little Kevin says, as he runs and jumps into Sarah's arms.
"Group hug," says little Kevin as they all laugh and embrace. Oh, the love of family, how beautiful it is. The Gallaghers would lean on that love from one another in the coming days!! Whether your farming in rural New Brunswick, or walking down a city street in Los Angeles, California, trouble is always knocking on the door. For now, everything was going good, and hey it's almost summertime!!!

Frederick Demerchant

Miracle From First Pit Pond

Chapter 4: Smiles for a Big Trip

"Kevin, do you have any homework tonight?" asks Donna June.
"Yes, mama. I have spelling and three pages of reading to do for my reading class."
"Ok, go gather the eggs please, and I'll help you with your homework when you are done. How about you David?"
"I just have to finish my book report, should take about an hour, mom."
"Ok, go give the cows some water then come do your homework please."
"Ok mom," replies David.
"How about you Joseph?"
"No mame," he replies.
"Ok, can you go clean the big stalls for me?"
"Sure mom." David get's up and gives his mom a peck on the cheek as he walks out the door.
"What about you Sarah?" asks Donna June.
"No, mom," she replies. "I'll go help Joseph with the pig stalls."
"No you stay here please, your dad and I want to talk to you about something." They lay an envelope on the table with Sarah's name written on it.
"What's this?" asks Sarah.
"Open it and find out," replies her dad. A new ten dollar bill and four older ones are inside.
"There's $14 here, replies Sarah"
"That's right," says Donna June.
"What's it for?" asks Sarah.
"It is for your PEI trip!" replies her dad. Sarah puts it back in the envelope and says "No dad, you keep it for the farm."
"Hunny, do you remember the wood your dad had cut from our land last winter, and the pulpwood he cut?"

"Yes I do mama," replies Sarah.
"This money came all from the profits of the wood and some more to spare!! It wouldn't be right to send you to Prince Edward Island without some spending money, now would it?" asks her dad.
Sarah's eyes grow big and bright!
"Dad I thought you didn't have the extra money?"
"Well Sarah, thank the good Lord for Mr. Walker from Southwest Valley Forestry. We sold some cedar to them to help pay for your trip." Sarah runs to her dad and gives him a big old hug!
"Oh, daddy, daddy thank you so much," Sarah says.
"You're welcome sweetie: Michael smiles and says.
"Thank you mama!" Sarah runs over to her mom and gives her a big hug.
"You're welcome Sarah," says Donna June!!
"I've got the best parents in the world," Sarah smiles and says!"
"Well I would say we have a pretty good daughter too," Donna June smiles and replies.
"Amen to that!!!" says Michael.
"Oh mama and daddy, I'm so, so happy and excited!"
"Well that's good and you should be. Prince Edward Island is a beautiful place sweetheart."
"It is mama. You have been there?"
No your dad went there for four days and four nights . Yep we rented a cottage right on the beach on the ocean!! It was absolutely wonderful!!!"
"Wow it sounds amazing," says Sarah.
"It was," says herdad. "And now you will get to experience it this summer too."
"I can't wait!!" Sarah smiles and says.
"Another neat things about Prince Edward Island is the dirt there is red," says her father.
"Red?" asks Sarah.
"Yes, red," says her father. "You know how our dirt here is brown? Well over there it is red."
"Wow, I didn't know that," replies Sarah.
"Yep and those old potatoes over there just love that red dirt. They grow some of the best potatoes in the world over there!!" says her

dad. "Wish our potatoes on our farm was as good as theirs," replies her dad. Donna June winks and smiles and says "our potatoes are just fine sweetheart. Our third best vegetable seller three years in a row!"
Michael smiles "Hey Sarah that's right."
"How do you know that?" Asks her dad.
"Dad I'm gonna tell you what I tell my brother's all the time. I'm not just another pretty face! I'm quite knowledgeable!"
Donna June and Michael break out giggling!!!
"Well time to do some haying," Michaeal says. "I love you girls!!"
"We love you too dad," Sarah smiles and says.
"Hunny, I got an idea," says Donna June. "Why don't you go to your room and make a list of everything you wanna take with you on your Prince Edward Island trip and I'll review it with you, to make sure you don't forget anything."
"Good idea mama, but I can help you fix supper."
"No it's ok, I'll get supper if you go work on your list. Oh, but before you go, please grab the mayonnaise out of the fridge and set it on the table? I'm making chicken and homemade potato salad for supper." They both look at each other at the same time and blurt out "Kevin's favorite". They giggle together as Sarah runs up the stairs to her room. She thinks about all the things she will bring.
"Now I gotta write this list and have mama review it, and have supper dishes done up by 7 pm because we leave at 7:05 pm to make youth group for 7:30 pm." Sarah was a busy fourteen year old girl growing up in Southwest, NB, but probably most fourteen year old girls in Southwest, New Brunswick in 1985 were busy too. Sarah was as charming as she was tough. She knew she would have a great time over there, and who knows, maybe even meet a boy. As she began to write her list, she thought "wait a minute, this trip was about learning new things and fun and adventure, and well, who knew maybe even meeting a boy might be thrown into that mix." Sarah sighed and smiled as she wrote her list.

*****

The rumbling of the diesel tractor pulling up by the big, farm door. Joseph grabbed the handle and opened the big farm door up wide. "Hey," dad shouts out to Joseph. "Hey boys, how goes the battle?" Michael asks.
"Good daddy," says Kevin."My basket is so full I have to be careful when I set it down and grab another one, there's so many eggs the baskets can't handle them all!!!
"That's great son, good job!!!" says Micaeal.
"I guess the chickens are working overtime today," says Joseph.
"Hey how come everyone is standing around talking and I'm the only one working?" asks David.
"You're doing a fine job, carry on, carry on," replies Joseph. They all chuckle.
"We're just taking a break and talking to daddy," says Kevin. David rubs Kevin's head as he walks by.
"I know, I know I'm just razzing you guys," says David.
"Well my boys are doing such a great job. How about I run into the house and grab a picture of that homemade ice tea your mama makes."
"Now you're talking," says Kevin.
They all laugh. Michael jumps down off the tractor and heads for the farm house. As he walks along, he says a silent prayer. "God thanks for my boys and thanks for Sarah. and all the blessings you give us everyday. Please keep making a way for this farm. So that I can pay it off and one day leave it to my beautiful children, in Jesus' name, Amen."

Yes the love of family, truly a blessing whether a person chooses to realize it or not. The screen door gently shuts behind Michael. "Hunny could you whip up a fresh container of your homemade ice tea? We got some hard working thirsty boys out there."
"I made one a couple hours ago dear," says Donna June. "It should be nice and cold!"
"Thank you sweetheart!" says Michael As he walks back over to the boys, a lot of things cross Michael's mind. "Will it be a good summer for the farm? Will the large garden they always put in sell

out again? Will pork prices rise, fall, or stay the same?" Right now though something more important is taking place.
"Dad, dad, dad!!!" yells Sarah.
"Yes, hunny," he says as she catches up from behind him.
"You forgot the glasses."
"Oh, it's okay sweetheart. We have some styrofoam cups in the barn."
"Well i'm here with these ones now, so save your other ones."
As Saraha and Micaeal make their way into the barn. She pours her dad and all her brothers a nice cold drink of homemade ice tea.
"Jeez, sis talk about service," says Joseph.
"Hey dad just forgot the glasses Joseph," Sarah giggles and says.
"I love you Sarah" says Kevin.
"I love you too, Kevin," Sarah smiles and says.
"You're okay in my book too!" says David.
"Ha, ha, ha" they all laugh!
"Oh my boys, my boys," says Sarah.
"Hey we're mom's boys too!!" says Joseph.
"Oh I know," says Sarah. "I'm giving her a break."
Yes Sarah was the glue that held the Gallagher family together. The rock of jabalter you may say, or maybe a rose among the thorns of all those boys!!!

Frederick Demerchant

Chapter 5: PEI here we come

"Thanks for driving me over to the church Joseph. The school bus is picking us up at 10:00 am for our trip."
"You be careful over there sis."
"I will," says Sarah.
"But more than anything, have fun." Joseph drives away, then stops. He puts the car in reverse. "Hey Sarah."
"Yes, Joseph," she replies.
"Watch out for those PEI spuds. I hear they are monstrous!"
"Get out of here big brother!!" Sarah smiles and says.
Joseph slowly pulls away. Sarah shouts out with a loud voice.
"Hey Joseph!" He hits the breaks. "Yea," he says.
"I love you big brother!"
"I love you too lil sis,'' he replies.
"And we love you too Sarah." Sarah turns around and smiles at three beautiful smiling familiar faces: Emma Melanson, Krista Davenport, and Darren Nicols. Three good friends and classmates of Sarah's. Sarah smiles "thanks, Darren,"
"Every world of it is true," says Emma.
"And I think you're okay too," says Krista. They all laugh!
So Sarah says, "Darren. Are you all psyched about our big, Prince Edward Island class trip?"
"Excited, excited? Well let's put it this way. Like my brothers attack the Christmas turkey at high noon at my house on Christmas day, that's what I would compare it to," Saraha smiles and says.
"Whoa!!! That's pretty excited," Krista says.
"Ha, ha ,ha," they all share a good laugh together!
"I was there once when I was with my grandma for three days in August once," says Emma. "How about you Darren?'' Emma asks.
"No, I have never been," says Darren.

"I haven't either," says Krista.
"Well I was very young," said Emma, "but from what I remember, it was very, very beautiful!!!"
"Hey here's the bus," says Krista.
"PEI here we come," says Darren.
"The place will never be the same!" says Krista.
"Ha, ha, ha, ha," they all laugh.
"I wonder if their clams there are as good as they are here?" says Emma.
"I would think so," says Darren.
"They are still from the Bay of Fundy," says Krista.
"Well we will just have to order some and find out."
"I got $9," says Emma.
"I got $17," says Krista.
"I got $14," says Saraha.
"I got $20, oh plus $2 from my grandma," says Darren.
"Well looks like we will have treats all week." The value of youthful friendship; something that's good and pure!!!

The bus releases it's airbrakes and moves forward. "Attention class of grade 8. Your chariot of fire for Prince Edward Island is now departing." A rush of shouts and cheers are herald by twenty three kids, one teacher, two chaperones, and one parent. Dreams are coming true for this bunch, and dreams are precious like silver or an emerald stone.

****

Meanwhile back at the house, Donne June answers a telephone call.
"Hello?"
"Hello, Mrs. Gallagher?"
"Yes," replies Donna June.
"This is Allison Johnson of the girl guides group of Canada."
"Yes," says Donna June.
"How much do you charge per pie to make?"
"Oh it's $5.50 per pie."

"Is that so," replies Allison Johnson. "Well could I place an order for forty five pies? But I will pay you $6.25 per pie."
"Well that's very generous of you Allison, but I only charge $5.50 per pie. Why do you want to pay $33.75 more?"
"We are raising money to take the girls to a wilderness retreat lodge in Canose, New Brunswick. We already have orders for twenty nine pies, and three other people have expressed interest. So we are having a car wash Saturday June 4th, 9am-6pm. We are gonna have some pies for sale there too, but people are paying $9.50 per pie from us that gives us a profit of $146.25. That's almost half the cost of the wilderness retreat. Your pies are the talk of the town!! We don't mind cutting you in for some extra profit. You making them for us is a big help to our organization!"
"Well that's very kind and generous of you," replies Donna June. Things are looking up for the Gallagher family.
"Ok, Donna June, that's fifteen lemon merangine, fifteen apple, ten chocolate cream, two banana cream, and three peach."
"Okay, they will be ready by 6:00pm, June 3rd."
"Ok, thank you Donna June," replies Allison.
"You're welcome, God bless you Allison."
"God bless you too," replies Allison to Donna June.

****

"So Sarah, did you know that PEI was where Confederation was born for our country?"
"Yes I did. I remember that from social studies class."
"How exciting!!" says Emma. "We are going to see the place where it all started for our country."
As the bus rolled along on the outskirts of Cambridge Narrows, New Brunswick with the kids in route for beautiful Prince Edward Island. Sarah looked out the window and thought to herself "every mile I roll along it's closer to PEI. What would it be like?" she wondered. "It can't be that different," she thought. But then again they have red dirt there, and that isn't something she has seen before. "Perhaps I'll see lots of things I have never seen before." Her thoughts are interrupted by one of the chaperones.
"Ok kids, we are gonna stop at the store in Sailsbury. That's the only stop before the ferry to Prince Edward Island."

"Sarah, I'm going in for a pepsi. Can I get you anything?"
"A pepsi," Sarah thinks "would be nice."
"Here Emma, let me get you some money, and you can get me one as well!"
"No, no, no," says Emma. "This one is on me!"
Sarah smiles and says thank you! She stood up to stretch, she thought to herself "how lucky she was!! Good friends, a great family, and being on an adventure!! What else could a young lady ask for? Well, perhaps maybe meeting a nice boy in Prince Edward Island. Someone to share some time with, and maybe get a lifelong friend and pen pal out of it to!" Her thoughts are interrupted again by Emma.
"Here ya go, my friend! A nice cold one for you!"
"Thank you Emma," says Sarah.
"You know Sarah, I was thinking in the store, we should go looking for sea glass, when we get to PEI!"
"What exactly is sea glass?" Sarah asks.
"Well I'm not sure if it is actual broken glass, from bottles that have been in the ocean for many years, or if it is a natural thing from the ocean. But it comes in many different colors, and sizes. I once read in a book how a lady in Chicago went to different beaches and collected it. On the Atlantic Ocean and the Pacific Ocean. She used some sort of special glue and made a small coffee table out of it, and it was very beautiful! It had so many different colors that seemed to all blend together,"
"Wow, that's great!!" said Sarah. "You know Emma," said Sarah. "God loves us so much, he gave us so many different colors to enjoy!! Think of the rainbow. A promise to us, that he will never destroy the earth again by water and he gave us all the colors of the bow to tell us that."
"Very interesting," Emma said. "I've never thought of it that way! God gives us other colorful good things too," Sarah says!
"What's that?" asks Emma.
"The blue in the sky, the colors of the hardwood leaves in the fall, and a colorful friend like you!"
"Aw, thanks," Emma smiles and says. "Soon we will be on that ferry boat" says Emma."

"Yes we will my friend," says Saraha.
Darren walks over to Sarah and sits down. "Hey Sarah did you know that PEI once had an active railroad from one end of the island to the other?"
"No, I didn't," says Sarah.
"I read it in a book. I believe it was last year that they tore up the last section of track."
"Wow, so many things she was learning about the island before they even got there."
"Now how did that peak your interest?" Sarah asks Darren.
"Well as you probably are aware of, railways are what helped to form, shape and connect our country coast to coast, but it brought a lot of prosperity to our home province of New Brunswick. But I found it fascinating how the smallest province totally only accessible by boat or airplane had an active railway system!!"
"I can see why you found it interesting the more I think about it, the more fascinating it sounds!" said Emma.
"Yes." The kids laughed and giggled and talked as the miles rolled on by. In what seemed like no time at all, a loud voice caught everyone's attention as the lady entered the bus.
"Grade eight class, I'm Rhonda Coleson from Marine Atlantic. Just a few safety rules to go over before you drive onto the ferry. Exit once the traffic officer on the ferry tells you to. Once you go upstairs, you're not allowed back downstairs on the bus, so take your wallets and purses with you. If you go outside on the top deck, hold onto the safety rail along the edge. And most importantly enjoy your time on Prince Edward Island!"
The bus erupts with a big roar of cheer!!! Rhonda Coleson smiles and waves as she gets off the bus.

The long drive was over and a new and exciting ferry ride to a world of wonder. Prince Edward Island.
"I hear sometimes you can look down off the ferry and see big jellyfish floating by," says Emma to Sarah.
"Really?" asks Sarah. "That would be neat to see."
Krista and Darren show up smiling and say "well we made it everybody."
"Yes we did," Emma smiles and replies.

"I bet we will look back at different times through our lives and remember this trip," says Darren.

"I'm sure we will," says Sarah.

"I hope time just creeps," says Darren "because I'm sure we are going to be having so much fun!".

The traffic officer steps into the bus and says, "please exit single file, one at a time and have fun kids. A world of wonder now awaits!"

Chapter 6: Saraha makes two new Friends

After a nice ferry ride across the Atlantic ocean, they arrive where they are staying. Golden Beach Cabins.
"Welcome to Golden Beach Cabins," says a smiling young check in agent. Sarah and Emma walk behind Anne Miller. Troy Miller's mom who was a chaperone, and they gaze in wonder. A wall full of pictures of past guests.
"Wow look at this one," says Sarah.
"A guy holding a trophy and this one a little boy holding a fish as big as him. This one, a lady holding a vase of pretty flowers," says Emma.
"Oh, I see you have found our wall of fame," says a lady wearing a name tag that says Pearl. "I am Pearl, nice to meet ya's," she smiles and says as she shakes the young lady's hands.
"Who is the lady with the vase of flowers?" asks Emma.
"That is Mrs. Joan Donaldson. She is from Ontario and came to PEI for a week to host "Decorate your life with Flowers". It was a huge success!! Two hundred and seventy-five people attended from as far away as Spain to use flowers indoors and outdoors to brighten their lives."
"Wow," says Emma "that's so cool!!"
"I'll say," Sarah smiles and replies.
"Yes it was cool," replies Pearl.
"Who is the man holding the trophy?" asks Sarah.
"That's Mr. Stephen O'Donell. Three time world PGA tour champion from Dublin, Ireland. He always heard how nice the golf courses were here, so he came and stayed a week here with us, golfing all over the Island at four different golf courses."

"Wow," replies Sarah.
"And who is this little boy with a fish bigger than him?" asks Emma.
"That is Michael David Johnson. An inner city little boy from Chicago who had never ever seen the ocean or had been out of the big city before. He came here on a week exchange program for country kids to go to a big city and inner city kids to go to the country. He had a blast! Charlie, the cabin's owner, took him deep sea fishing. This is a picture of him with his catch. It's an 82 lb 4ft 5 inch long cod fish. Ha, ha, ha" laughs Pearl. "Michael was ten years old and 4'7'' tall."
"So he was a little bit bigger than the fish," replies Emma.
"Yeah, a whole two inches," smiles Sarah and says.
"That's right," replies Pearl.
"Wow, so awesome!" says Emma.
Soft beautiful music from Bach is playing in the background. Pearl puts her arms around each of the girls. "We try our best here to make each guest feel loved and welcome" she smiles and says. "It's maybe what you would say is a little bit of Prince Edward Island hospitality to everyone."
"I think that's great," says Sarah.
"Hey, thanks," replies Pearl.
"No I mean it," Sarah says. "We need more love and kindness in the world today. God bless you Pearl and thanks for doing your part," Sarah smiles and sticks out her hand. "I'm Sarah, Sarah Gallagher." Pearl smiles and shakes her hand. "I'm Pearl Adams, and the pleasure is all mine, miss Gallagher."
This joyous official meeting by Pearl and Sarah with the beautiful Bach music playing in the background is quickly and loudly interrupted by noise of confusion and chaos!!
"Dad I have two barbies with me. I packed them under my sweaters to keep them protected."
"Oh, that's crazy talk, Katie, nothing would happen to them anyway! Just because you don't take extra precautions to protect what's precious to you." "Don't ridicule me because I do Brett."
"Oh, you're crazy, Katie,'' says Brett.

"Kids, kids!!!" A man cries out in distress! "Please stop arguing," as he walks through the door with two travel bags over his shoulder, a suitcase in one hand and little Katie holding his other. Pearl smiles and says "Hi, welcome to Golden Beach Cabins."
"Oh, hi," the man replies and smiles in spite of all the craziness. Sarah walks over and says "you kinda look like you got a big load on you, let me take those travel bags from off your shoulder for you."
"Oh, how kind of you young lady," the man sticks out his hand and smiles. "I'm Larry, Larry Nicols."
"Hi, Mr. Nicols, it's a pleasure to meet you. I'm Sarah, Sarah Gallagher. It is a pleasure to meet you sir! And this young lady here is my friend Emma."
"Hey,'' Emma says as she smiles and waves.
"This young man here is my son Brett and this is my daughter Katie. And the other young man coming through the door with the other suitcases is my son, Jeff."
"Well let's get everyone checked in," Pearl smiles and says.
"Pearl, why don't you check in Mr. Nicols and his family first," says Sarah.
"Oh, no, you were here first," says Larry to Sarah.
"It's okay Mr. Nicols. You look a little stressed out and tired," Sarah replies.
Mr. Nicols smiles and replies " two days of hard driving from Toronto, so I guess you could say I am a little."
"Well go ahead," Sarah says.
"Thanks," Larry smiles and says to Sarah.
"You're welcome," Sarah smiles and says.
"Ok here we are," Pearl smiles and says "reservations for Brett, Jeff, Katie, and Larry Nicols."
Jeff puts his hand on his dad's shoulder "ok dad, your vacation officially starts now."
Sarah smiles at Jeff. He smiles back at her with his big brown eyes and chestnut brown hair. "Time to decompress and enjoy yourself," Jeff says to his dad.
"Yes, yes, it is son," Larry smiles and says.
"What do you do for work up in Toronto?" Sarah asks.

"Oh I have a great job but a very stressful one," Larry smiles and says.
"A very stressful one," Jeff replies.
"Larry smiles and says "I'm an NHL scout for the Toronto Maples Leafs."
"Wow what a cool job," replies Emma.
"Yep, it's definitely cool, but it wears on ya," Larry smiles and says.
"How so?" asks Emma.
"Well dad has to find new talent for the leafs, and try to get them molded and ready for all season. And then hopefully to take them into the playoffs."
"Wow that's so cool!" replies Emma.
"I'll say," Sarah smiles and replies.
"Yes," says Jeff, "but not easy."
"Here you go Mr. Nicols," replies Pearl. "Cabin number eight."
"Thank you," replies Larry. They grab their luggage and walk away. Just before they go through the door, Larry stops and turns around and says "Hey Sarah."
"Yes Mr. Nicols," she replies.
"Why don't you and Emma join us tonight for some smores and hot dogs around the campfire tonight, for the kindness you showed to us in letting us check in first." Sarah looks at Emma, Emma smiles back at Sarah.
"We would be honoured to sir," Sarah says.
"Well lovely," Larry says "see you girls tonight at 9 pm, cabin number eight."
The Nicols family retrieved their luggage and walked out the door.
"Wow did you see how cute Jeff was?" asks Emma to Sarah.
Sarah smiles and blushes a little.
"I think he likes you to."
Sarah says to Emma, "why would you say that?"
"I don't know, I just have a feeling," Emma smiles and replies.
"Great job passing on that kindness," Pearl smiles and says.
"Thanks so much," says Emma.
"There you go girls, cabin number twenty-four for you! I'm sure you guys will find it comfy and cozy."

Miracle From First Pit Pond

"Just the way we love it," replies Emma.
"Thank you," says Sarah.
Pearl smiles and hands Emma the key. "You ladies are most welcome."

Well after a great supper of PEI fish and chips, a PEI speciality, the grade eight class is enjoying an evening stroll on the beach.
"Wow listen to the surf roll in."
"I know it's so beautiful," says Emma to Darren.
"Do you know what I was just thinking about?" says Sarah to Darren.
"What's that?" asks Darren.
"Look how God made everything so similar, and yet so different. The surf rolls into the shore and then it comes back out again. Like we have Sunday, then a long week but Sunday always comes back again."
"Yes," says Darren and it's a lot like the seasons. We have newness of spring, then the warmth of summer, and then the leaves of fall in the fall, and then a cold winter. But spring is just around the corner and it always comes back."
"Wow, a very interesting take," replies Emma.
"Well as I'm enjoying the time here with you guys and I look and listen to the surf, it makes me thankful."
"Thankful for what?" asks Emma.
"That God is big enough to make all this, yet small enough to know us all deeply and intimately."
"I'm thankful for all of it," replies Emma: the moments of each day, and the beauty of the earth, and the stars in the sky. By the way, there are a lot of them out tonight," replies Emma.
"Well I'm thankful for two things," says Darren.
"What's that?" asks Emma.
"I'm thankful for my big comfy bed in my room in my cabin, and I'm thankful to God for you guys as well!!!"
"We are thankful for you too Darren," replies Sarah.
"We sure are!" says Emma.
"Well on that note, I feel that big comfy bed calling me. Goodnight my friends."
"Goodnight!" Reply Sarah and Emma.

"What time is it?" Sarah asks.
"It's 8:55pm."
"Time we was walking down to Mr. Nichols' cabin," says Sarah.
"I hope Mr. Nichols feels better, he looked pretty stressed out to me," says Sarah.
"I'm sure he will," says Emma.
"Who wouldn't feel more relaxed in this beautiful place?" asks Emma.
"That's true," Sarah replies.
As they walk down towards cabin number eight, they see the flow of a campfire. Mr. Nichols was relaxed all right. He had a cold glass of ice tea in one hand and a flaming marshmallow in the other. As he sees the girls coming, he smiles and waves.
"Hi girls. I'm glad ya's made it."
"Thanks Mr. Nichols," replies Sarah.
"Hello ladies. Nice to see ya's.:
"Hi Jeff," says Emma.
"Hi Jeff," replies Sarah.
"Where are Katie and Brett?" Emma asks.
Larry chuckles. "Well when they finally got done arguing, they played on the beach together for a couple hours then they each had a shower and hit the hay!"
"I guess the arguing really plays them out hey dad?" Replies Jeff.
"Well how old are your children Mr. Nichols?" asks Emma.
"Brett is eleven, Katie is nine, and big bad Jeff here is sixteen." Mr. Nichols smiles and says "yes, kids will be kids but I love them!"
"And we love you too dad!" says Jeff.
"So where is Mrs. Nichols?" asks Emma. "Did she have to work and couldn't come?"
"No," says Mr. Nichols. "Unfortunately I am divorced."
"Oh, I am so, so sorry," replies Emma.
"Oh thanks," replies Larry "very, very kind of you. Yes it's been almost five years now. But hey, I got my three rugrats that I love and adore!"
"And we adore you too, dad!"
"Hey, thanks son," Larry smiles and says.

"Here you go Sarah, a hot smore for you," says Jeff. "And one for you Emma."
"Thanks, Jeff," the girls say in unison.
Mr. Nicols is standing there with a cold glass of ice tea for each of the girls.
"Here you go girls, some ice tea to wash down your smores."
"Thanks," the girls reply.
"Mr. Nicols, if you don't mind me saying, you look a lot less stressed," says Sarah.
"Ohhh I am," Larry smiles and says. "You gotta love these maritime vacations!!"
"Oh, you have been to the maritimes before?" asks Emma.
"Oh yes," Larry smiles and says. "This is my third PEI vacation. I've been to Halifax once and New Brunswick twice."
"Really? That's where we are from," replies Sarah..
"Oh yeah, cool!" Replies Larry. "I really love the maritimes, " replies Larry.
"Thanks," says Emma.
"Like Jeff told you earlier, my job is very, very, stressful at times."
"Have you ever thought of giving it up?" asks Emma.
"No," replies Mr. Nicols. "I love being a scout and the good outweighs the bad and besides the Leafs aren't gonna be in a slump forever."
Everyone at the campfire breaks out laughing.
"Yes I believe we will obtain the Stanley Cup again!"
"Hey Sarah, why don't you tell Mr. Nicols about your brother David? He is really, really good," replies Emma.
"That's for sure," says Sarah.
"Oh, interesting," says Mr. Nicols. "Which JR team does he play for? Edmonston, Fredericton, Moncton?"
"No he doesn't play for any junior team," says Emma.
"Ummm, I thought you said he was really good?"
"He is," replies Sarah. "But he doesn't play for the junior team, he plays on First Pit Pond."
"What is First Pit Pond?" asks Mr. Nicols.
"It's not a what, it's a where," replies Emma.
"My brother plays hockey on a frozen pond not far from our farm. It's a logging road. The logging road has two gravel pits on it. The

first pit is the one closest to our place, and there is a pond beside it so we call it First Pit Pond.

"Interesting," replies Jeff.

"Jeez I don't know Sarah. A pond and not a junior team," says Mr. Nicols.

"Well dad, I don't know," says Jeff. "Rocket Richard, Bobby Hull, and Bobby Orr all got their starts on frozen ponds as well."

"I tell you what," Emma says to Mr. Nicols. "If you see his swirling shot, you may think differently."

"Swirling shot? What is a swirling shot?" asks Larry.

"Well you see, my brother has been watering our cows forever," says Sarah. "When you dump the water in the trough with one foul swoop a lot of times you get splash back. Now in summer, spring or fall, it isn't too bad. But when you are in the barn in the winter, it's cold enough as it is. My brother developed a swirling technique to keep the water from splashing up."

"And he has somehow implemented it into a hockey shot?" asks Mr. Nicols.

"Wow, cool!" says Jeff.

"Interesting," says Mr. Nicols.

"Hey Larry and Jeff, we are going for a late night stroll on the beach. Would you guys like to come?" Asks Mr. and Mrs. Davidson from cabin number twelve. Friends of theirs that they made by staying there over the years.

"Ohhh we would love to," says Larry "but Brett and Katie are asleep.

"You go ahead dad," replies Jeff. "I'll stay with them.

"Are you sure son?" asks Larry.

"Emma would you and Sarah like to join us?"

"I'd love to," replies Emma.

"Umm I think I will stay and keep Jeff company," says Sarah..

"Ok, we will be back in a half an hour," Emma grins and waves bye.

"Dad is such a great father to us Sarah," says Jeff.

"That's great Jeff," Sarah smiles and says "I was very sorry to hear of your mom and dad's divorce. That had to be very, very, tough on everybody."

"Yes, it is," says Jeff. "I thank God that he helps us all to cope."
"Don't ever forget Jeff, God cares. God loves and God's always there to hear your prayer."
"I know Sarah. Thank you," says Jeff. "Mom left dad for another man when I was ten. Brett and Katie were just small. And a year later, dad got served with divorce papers."
"I'm so sorry," says Sarah. "Do you get to see your mom often?"
"No," replies Jeff. "When she left, she not only left dad, but she left us. But hey, like I said I thank God everyday for my dad."
"And you should," Sarah smiles and says.
"And do you know what?" Asks Sarah to Jeff.
"What's that Sarah?" replies Jeff.
"I believe God will reward your dad for loving his kids and doing what's right."
"Really?" asks Jeff.
"Oh, for sure," says Sarah.
"Maybe he will reward him by letting the Leafs win a cup soon."
"Well you never know," Sarah smiles and says.
"Your brother sounds like he has developed some interesting techniques."
"Yeah, he's quite innovative at hockey, that's for sure."
"You know what Sarah? I got a feeling your brother would really go for it if given a shot."
"It has always been his dream to play in the NHL," Sarah says.
Jeff pulls out his wallet, "Here Sarah, here is one of my dad's business cars."
"Thanks,"replies Sarah.
"Take good care of it. Maybe you can call him and arrange for him to come down and see your brother in action, next winter."
"Do you think he would come?" Asks Sarah.
"Sure, talent is what the Leafs need and he's the man in charge of that."
"So glad I met you Sarah!"
"Me too," Sarah replies. Jeff gives Sarah a hug, and a kiss on the cheek," Sarah smiles.
"Hey, how about another smore?" Jeff asks.
"Sounds wonderful," replies Sarah.

As Jeff and Sarah stare up at the stars in the nighttime sky. Sarah thinks how this night is so nice and peaceful. And how she likes her two new friends, Jeff and his dad. As they eat two more smores, and share some laughs, Emma and Larry return.
"Hey guys, how are ya's?" asks Larry.
"Fine," Jeff replies.
"How was the walk guys?" asks Sarah.
"Just beautiful! So many stars out tonight," says Emma.
"Yes, they're beautiful," says Larry.
"Well son, I'm gonna turn in."
"Me too," says Emma.
"Me as well," Sarah says.
"Thanks for a great evening Mr. Nicols," says Emma.
"Thank you girls," says Larry.
"Goodnight everyone."
"Goodnight," says Jeff.
"See ya's tomorrow," says Emma.

As one day ended and another began so went forth the students to board the bus back for home. But each and everyone of them had a lovely class trip.
"Well Sarah and Emma, it was great to get to know ya's. I hope you have a safe trip back," says Jeff.
"Me too," says Mr. Nicols.
"Aww, thanks," the girls say.
"Oh, and Sarah."
"Yes Jeff?" Sarah says.
"Don't forget to write and take good care of that thing I gave you."
"I will take care of it and I will write," Sarah smiles and says.
As the girls board the bus, Darren looks at his two friends. "Was this a great trip or what?"
"Absolutely," says Sarah.
"And someone met a boy," Emma smiles and says.
"Oh good for you, Sarah," says Darren.
"You are gonna write him and be pen pals right Sarah?" asks Emma.
"Most definitely," Sarah smiles and says, "most definitely."

Chapter 7: Summer turn to Fall, Fall turns to Winter

"Joseph, Joseph."
"Yes, mom."
"Can you get your father please and tell him to come in the house, he has an important phone call."
"Sure can, mom," Joseph replies.
"Oh, and Joseph, it's 4:07 pm, have David, Sarah and Kevin come in and you as well in exactly twenty minutes. We have to get cleaned up, eat and dressed for the Christmas pageant at church tonight."
"Ok mom, I will." Joseph goes to the back of the barn where Michael is working on a hydraulic line on the tractor.
"Dad," say's Joseph.
"Yes, son?"
"Mom wants you to go in the house right away, you have an important phone call."
"Ok son, thank you."
As Michael makes his way into the farmhouse Donna June looks at him and smiles.
"Who is it?" he asks.
"You will see," she smiles and says. Michael grabs the phone receiver.
"Hello?"
"Hello Michael, how are you doing?"
"Good thanks, and yourself?"
"Just fine, thanks."
"It's Tim Walker from Southwest Valley Forestry calling."

"Yes sir, I recognize your voice. Nice to talk to you."
"You as well, sir," says Mr. Walker.
" I was wondering if you and your son Joseph would be interested in cutting some pulpwood for us this winter?"
"Well Mr. Walker, my son Joseph is leaving on January third for four months. He is going all the way to Timmins, Ontario."
"Timmins, Ontario? What on earth is he gonna do all the way out there?" Mr. Walker asks.
"Well he read in a popular mechanics magazine that there is a welding shop in Timmins, Ontario looking for people wanting to learn to weld. They pay his flight from Fredericton, and his flight back home, in May. Put him up in staff housing and feed him and pay him a styphing of $65 per week. He just has to work from 8am till 6pm five days a week. Over and above that he can work Saturdays a straight rate of $8.65 per hour. From 6 am till close at 6:00pm."
"8.65 per hour, " says Mr. Walker, not bad at all for someone learning how to weld."
"Not bad at all," replies Micheal. "All his hours will go towards his certification as well. SO when he starts in community college next September, he will already have the basics down and so many working hours completed."
"Well I am very happy and excited for him," replies Mr. Walker.
"Well thanks alot sir, we are as well. It really works out great for everyone. He has decided he wants to stay on and help run the farm, but he wants something to fall back on. And with farming we can certainly put his new welding skills to good use.
"Absolutely," replies Mr. Walker.
"But don't worry, Mr Walker. I have been talking to my neighbour, Winston Short. He got laid off his golf course job as of November 3rd. And he doesn't start back till April 20th. He asked me if I had any extra work. I told him maybe a possibility of cutting pulpwood for Southwest Valley Forestry. He said that would be great and if it comes through, he would work for me so I can hire him."
"Well wonderful," replies Mr. Walker. "We are winding down for Christmas, but how about I stop by your place 8:00 am on

December 27th for you to sign our standard contractor winter contract papers?"

"Absolutely sir, sounds great! I'll have the tea kettle on."

"Sounds wonderful," replies Mr. Walker.

"Oh, and Michael."

"Yes, Mr. Walker?"

"Yes if your wife had one of those apple or peach pies kicking around that day, oh man I would be appreciative."

"I think something can be arranged," Michael smiles and says."

"That would be great," says Mr. Walker.

"I had two slices of her apple pie at the community hunters supper on October 27th. Now let me tell you what young man, that was two pieces of heaven on earth."

"Thanks, Mr. Walker. Very kind of you." says Michael.

"Oh Michael, one more thing. It's Thursday December 22nd. Could you stop by my office tomorrow morning anytime between 7:30 and 9:30 am? The company and I have a little something for you here."

"Ok Mr. Walker, no problem and thank you."

"Oh and Michael, Merry Christmas to you and that fine family of yours in case I forget to tell you tomorrow."

"Thanks, Mr. Walker, and a very Merry Christmas to you as well sir!! Ohhh and to Mrs. Walker as well!"

"Bye, bye now."Goodbye Michael." Michael hangs up the phone and puts his arm around Donna June.

"Honey, I love you!" Donna gives him a kiss, "I love you too. Good phone call?" she smiles and asks.

"It was great! Mr. Walker wants more pulpwood cut this winter."

"That's great honey!" replies Donna June.

"Yes, the farm had a good summer and fall, and now with wood to cut this winter, it will be even better. Oh honey, by the way, Mr. Walker is stopping over at 8am Tuesday December 27th with the winter contract agreement for cutting the wood. I told him I would have the teapot on. He wanted to know if you could make either one of your apple pies or peach pies so he would have a slice."

"I think something can be arranged," Donna June giggles and says. "How about I make one of each and Mr. Walker can have a slice of each."

Michael asks her, "how did I get so lucky anyway?"
"Every good gift and every perfect gift is from above. And cometh down from the father of lights with whom is no variableness, neither shadow of turning." Michael smiles and says "ahh that's how I got so lucky."
"You got it," says Donna June.
"James chapter 1 and verse 17 if my memory serves me right?"
"You got it again!" Donna June smiles and says.
All of a sudden all four Gallagher children burst through the door. Sarah hands a gift to her dad. David hands a gift to his mom. Joseph smiles and says "ok everybody, ready?"
"Yep," Kevin calls out and with the voice of an angel, Kevin Gallgher starts to sing.
"The Stars up in the Sky"
"The snow on the field
The warmth of a fire. The harvest giving a great yield."
Then Sarah and Joseph and David all join in with young Kevin as well and start to sing.
"It reminds us of Christmas. Of mama and daddy and their love. It reminds us of peace on earth. How Jesus came from above. To a little lowly manger
In a place called Bethlehem.
To give us the very best gift salvation
To give us the very best gift salvation."

Kevin sings the second verse in his sweet tenor voice.

Mama and daddy we thank you for being like the baby in the manger everyday you help guide us like the saviuor does. Everyday you remind us you're always here for us to. You remind us with love. And with faith we can accomplish what we set out to do.

As this joyous singing is taking place. Donna has her head against Micheal's chest as a tear falls from her eyes. Micheal is smiling ear to ear with a tear falling from his eye. All the children are singing the chorus again.

Miracle From First Pit Pond

It reminds us of Christmas.
Of mama and daddy and their love.
It reminds us of peace on earth and how Jrsus came from above.
To a little lowly manger. In a place called Bethlehem.
To give us the very best gift salvation, to give us the very best gift, salvation.

Kevin's sweet tenor voice belts out the last two bars of the song

To give us the very best gift salvation,
To give us the very best gift salvation.

Donna June and Michael quickly jump to their feet and clap and applaud. Donna June quickly runs to Joseph in one arm and Kevin in the other.
Sarah and David are quickly embraced by their father. As Donna June hugs Joseph and Kevin, she then runs over to Michael and waits to hug David and Sarah. As Joseph and Kevin walk over to their dad he quickly embraces them. After he hugs them he says "boys and Sarah, that was just wonderful!!!"
"Yes," says Donna June, "so beautiful!!!"
"Where did you kids ever hear it?" Donna June asks.
"Mama that's the best part of all," says Kevin.
"It's a Gallagher original."
"Joseph wrote it!!!" Donna June looks over at Joseph and lovingly smiles. Joseph was a young man of big strong stature. But he had a heart of gold like all the Gallagher children.
Donna June says to Joseph "Always remember son, you can do anything, and that song is beautiful!!!"
"She's right big brother, it's beautiful!!!" replies David as he grabs big Joseph in an embrace.
Sarah smiles and says "do you guys got room for your lil sister here?"
They both smile and reach out and draw Sarah into the embrace.
As Kevin is being lovingly held in his daddy's arm, Michael puts his other arm around Donna June.
"Merry Christmas everyone!" says Kevin.
"Merry Christmas Gallagher family," Donna June smiles and says.

Now the Gallaghers had three cords of softwood and four cords of hardwood to heat their farmhouse this winter. But if you could have bottled up all the heat from all the love in that farmhouse that night, you wouldn't have needed one stick of firewood for the next three winters.
"Mama, guess what?" says Kevin.
"What's that sweetie?" asks Donna June.
"I am so glad Christmas falls on Sunday this year, because Christmas Eve service will be fun, then on Jesus' birthday, after we open our gifts, we will go to church again to celebrate Him."
"Do you know what I think?" says Sarah.
"What," says Kevin.
"I think Jesus would be very proud of you for saying that!!" David smiles and says and with that into the church Christmas Pageant. The Gallaghers had a great Christmas. Mr. Walker came on the 27th and had the contract signed as he said. And he was ever so grateful that a warm piece of apple pie with a scoop of vanilla ice cream was waiting for him. And he was even more grateful that he was walking out the door with a whole peach pie, all for his own!!
"Thanks so much Donna June," replies Mr. Walker.
"You are most welcome, enjoy."
"Oh I will," Mr. Walker smiles and says.
"Goodbye for now."
"Bye, Mr. Walker."
Michael and Donna June stand in the doorway of their home, and wave him off. Yes life was floating along pretty good for the Gallagher family.
"Well, sweetheart, back to the barn for me," says Michael.
"Michael," Donna June smiles and says. "Yes dear," Michael replies.
"Sit down here for a minute." Michael scratches his head and says, "okay dear take my hand and bow your head please."
"Ok," Michael replies. Donna June begins to pray. "Dear Jesus, thank you for a good year, this year. Thank you that you always meet and exceed our needs. And thank you for my husband and children. In Jesus' name, Amen."

"Amen," says Michael. "I love you Donna June," Michael smiles and says.
"I love you too sweetheart," says Donna June.
Michael says, "your new Christmas sweater looks nice on you!"
"Thanks!" replies Donna June.
"Thank you for your love sweetheart." Donna winks and says.
Michael opened the front door to go to the barn where all the children were out doing their chores.
"I'm gonna go over the tractor really good today. Winston and I are gonna leave for Line Operation road at 7:30 am tomorrow morning with the tractor, to get logging."
"Ok, I'll come get ya at high noon for lunch tomorrow," Donna June smiles and says.
"Ok, Clint Eastwood," Michael laughs and says.
"Going to work, love ya," Michael says as he walks out the door.

Frederick Demerchant

Chapter 8: Pulp hooks, Hockey sticks and a Phone call

"Man, it sure is a frosty cold one, today Winston."
"It sure is Michael."
"Good thing we got those hot water couplers on your half ton and tractor or I'm afraid this old girl would never start."
"Yes, it's almost too cold to work today," says Michael.
"Oh, it's only -32C this morning."
"Only!!!" Michael laughs and says. "Well the limbs come off the spruce nice and easy in this weather," replies Winston.
"That's for sure," says Michael.
"You know, I heard on the news last night that this is the fourth coldest February since the turn of the century," says Michael.
"Wow, I didn't know that," says Winston.
"Well this thing has been recycling hot water through now for twenty-eight minutes," says Michael to Winston, "what do you say we give her a try?"
"Sure," says Winston.
With one little shot, the old tractor fired right up.

Meanwhile up at First Pit Pond, in comes Debbie Gardner with her station wagon. She parks and hollers to LeRoy and Marty.
"Boys, come home, it's too cold to play outside today."
"Oh mom, it's not that bad," says LeRoy.
David skates up and stops quickly, getting Debbie's bottom of her long coat sprayed with ice mist. "Hi, Mrs. Gardner, how are you?" asks David.
"David Gallagher, what are you guys doing on this pond today? You're gonna get frostbite!!!"

"It's not that bad if you stay moving Mrs. Gardner."
"You guys were out here till 9:30 last night," replies Debbie. "Now it's 8:45 am and you're out here again already."
"We have only been here an hour," says LeRoy.
"It is kinda chilly," says Stephen Theriault, in his full goalie gear."
"Yes it is," says Debbie. "Where is your snowmobile by the way?" asks Debbie.
"Oh it was too cold to start. So I crashed at David's last night. His parents and my parents said it was okay Mrs. Gardner."
"Well I think you should all come up to my house. I got a warm pot of Red River on the stove. It's a good morning to eat that and play board games."
"Awww mom do we have to?" asks Marty.
"Yes you do!" Replies Debbie.
"I don't see Darrell Cairns or Branden Copp or Peter Eales here this morning."
"Well Brandon is away at his grandma's for the weekend. And Darrell and Peter would have come today, but they said it was too cold."
"It is pretty chilly," says Stephen Theriault.
Mrs. Gardner sees David as he smiles.
"Mrs. Gardner you see I'm gonna be an NHL player and I'm taking Stephen with me. And if LeRoy and Maty keep practicing, they might have a shot as well! So you see, we gotta stay out here."
"Well until I see a signed letterhead offer from an NHL team, everyone of you, skates off and in the car." replies Debbie.
"Yes Mrs. Gardner," replies David.
"Arena ice will be a lot warmer than the pond, but I don't mind learning on the pond, it toughens me up for my conditioning in the NHL."
"David you sound so determined to reach this NHL dream you have," says Mrs. Gardner as they put the car into drive and began to ride to the Gardener's house.
David says "Oh, I'm gonna reach it."
"He is very, very good mom," says LeRoy.
"Well David, I hope God helps you achieve every dream you have."

Miracle From First Pit Pond

"Thanks Mrs. Gardner. I am gonna achieve it."
"Ok, boys," replies Mrs. Gardner, ``we are home. Boots off, wash up and I'll get you all a nice bowl of hot Red River cereal."
"Thank you, Mrs. Gardner," replies all the boys.
As the boys sit at the table and Debbie sets each bowl of cereal in front of them, David breaths in the sweet aroma of the steam coming up from the cereal.
"You know Mrs. Gardner," he says "I think a lot of you."
"Why thank you David," replies Debbie. "I think a lot of you too!"
"No , I mean it," says David. "You always take care of all of us kids, just like you do your own boys Marty and LeRoy, just like we were your own, you know. I'll never forget you when I get older."
Debbie smiles and looks down at him and says "thanks David that was very sweet of you, and do you know what young man?"
"What's that?" asks David. "I'll never forget you when you become the first National Hockey League player to come from St. Croix, New Brunswick."
"Population one hundred and twelve," shouts LeRoy.
They all share a laugh together. Yes, cold February days in New Brunswick, Canada, stiffens up the ice. But it's also a good day to sit around the family table, and play board games and share laughs as well.

Back down in the wood things are going good for Winston and Micheal. As the clock approaches 11:00 am, Micaeal asks, "what do you say Winston, we fall and limb four more spruce. Haul them out, buck them up into four feet wood then stop for lunch?"
"Yeah, sounds great," Winston smiles and says.
"Oh, by the way, last load I got a fire going, to eat our lunch. So we will have a nice warm fire to eat our lunch over."
"Ha, ha, ha, that's wonderful," replies Winston.
"Going out the door this morning my wife said she packed me ham and cheese today. But I think it will be ham and frozen brick cheese."
"Ha, ha, ha," both men chuckle and laugh.
"But I was thinking thanks to you and your fire, it will be ham and grill cheese."

"Yep," replies Mike, "with any luck at all, long range weather last night said warming up tomorrow afternoon to -11C and supposed to hover around there for a few days.
"Great for cutting and yarding pulp," Winston smiles and says.
"And great for playing hockey, too!" Winston says.
"There have been a lot of buzz around the community about your son, David."
"Oh, really?" asks Mike.
"He's really, really good, Mike! Maybe even good enough to make the pros."
"Really? Do you think so?" Asks Mike.
"I've never seen him play, but both my niece and nephew have. They say he's fast, very fast and stick handles great!"But what about his size? Asks Michael.
"Well what about it?" Asks Winston.
"Well he is just small to average in his build. I think my son Joseph would be more suitable in size to be a pro hockey player. Broad shoulders, tall and strong."
"Mike, don't forget dynamite comes in small packages," Winston smiles and says. "Remember Rocket Richard?" asks Winston. "He wasn't very big, but man could he play."
"Yes, he sure could," Michael smiles and says.
"Let's fall and limb these three," says Winston.
Yes the timber was harvested with a lot of ease on cold winter days. As they hauled the four trees out to the yard and bucked them up, Winston drives his pulp hook into a piece of pulp and began to pile. He says "you know Mike, my wife and I just have our one little girl, Michelle. But as she grows I'd try to help her," says Winston.
"What do you mean?" asks Mike.
"Well, she is only three years old," says Winston. But now take your David for example. He had great hockey ability. Have you ever thought of hiring a personal coach to work with David a couple of evenings a week?"
"I couldn't afford that right now," says Michael. "But my wife and I have tried to teach and raise them to be strong and stand tall."
"So what exactly do you mean by that?" Asks Winston.

"Well we have been a good example to them, and we have taught them to work hard. I believe if it's God's will for David to make the NHL, God will get him there."
"Winston smashes his pulp hook into the end butt of spruce.
"I believe he will too Mike, if it's His will for him, he will open the doors for David."
"And a door God opens, no man can shut." As he drives the last piece of pulp up into the pile.
"Now time for my ham and grilled cheese!!!" He smiles and says. Yes life wasn't all bad in Southwest New Brunswick. A little chilly but not all bad.

"So mom how many pie orders have you gotten since the new year? Have you been keeping track?" asks Sarah as she is working in the kitchen with her mom. As Sarah rolls out pie crust with a rolling pin that morning with her mom, Donna June says, " well I believe when these four are complete, it will make one hundred and seven in total since January first."
"Wow, that's great, mom." Sarah smiles and says. "And are you also counting the three you made on New Year's day as well?"
"Yes I am," says Donna June. "Mrs. Swim up the road, her husband and son and daughter always work on New Year's day."
"Yes, that's what you have to do when you're a nurse director and nurses at the manor."
"Yes, but she always has a New Year's supper cooked for them when she gets home too!" says Sarah to her mom. The Swim's were friends and neighbours to the Gallagher's. Mr. Swim took night courses to be a nurse, and his son and daughter followed suit. But Mrs. Swim had become one right out of high school. Mr. Swim used to be a planner in a Cedar Mill. The three pies made their New Year's supper. Donna was honoured to do it for them. The Gallaghers were greatly blessed to have good neighbours, such as was the Gardner family up the road as well. Debbie was a good lady who loved all the boys, just like her own two boys.
"Thanks, Mrs. Gardner," says Stephen."
"It is kinda chilly. We know, we know says David, you said that three or four times already," Debbie laughs and smiles at David.

"Guess what boys?" says Debbie. "I'll make my homemade stew and hot cocoa for lunch, how does that sound?"
"Well, ok Mrs. Gardner," says David, "you have a deal."
"Well lovely," says Mrs. Gardner.
LeRoy asks David, "David ever since I have known you, I believe you were four and I was six, all you have ever talked about is being an NHL player."
"Ya, I am gonna be," replies David.
"Well how are you gonna go about it?" Asks LeRoy.
"It isn't like they have open tryouts where you can just go and try out you know."
"I am determined," says David.
"Did you ever listen to Winston Churchill's speech on determination in World War II?" asks David to LeRoy. "We shall fight them in the air. We shall fight them on the land, we shall fight them in the street, we will never give up our island. And because of his determination, Britain is free and so are we!!!
LeRoy rolls his eyes "whatever ya think David," replies LeRoy.
"Yes sir, she's onward and upward for me," replies David. "And Stephen is gonna be a star goalie one day!"
"Ha, ha, ha, ha," laughs LeRoy.
"You're crazy," says LeRoy. "We are just kids on a pond."
"You'll see when I bring Lord Stanley's Cup to St. Croix, New Brunswick one day!!" David proudly smiles and says.

David if you ever bring Lord Stanley's Cup to St. Croix, NB. One day, I'll host the event."
"I'm holding you to that buddy," David smiles and says to LeRoy, "I'm holding you to that."
****
"Mom I just want you to know I love working in the kitchen with you making these pies!!!"
"Really, why is that? asks Donna June."
"Well," says Sarah. "I love my brothers, and I love my dad, but you know a little one on one girl time with you is great!!!"
"Well, sweetie, I feel the same way!!!" Donna June, smiles and says. "Let's celebrate our girl time by taking a break and having a hot cup of tea."

Miracle From First Pit Pond

"Sounds wonderful!!" Sarah replies. As they lay their rolling pins down, the phone rings on the wall.

"Hunny, will you grab that and I'll put on the tea," says Donna June.

"Sure, mom."

"Hello, Gallagher residence," Sarah smiles and says into the phone.

"Hi, is this Sarah?" the voice asks.

"Yes, this is Sarah" Sarah smiles and says.

"Sarah Gallagher from St. Croix, NB correct?"

"Yes, sir."

"Sarah Gallagher from route 630, Woodstock road, St. Croix, NB.

"Yup you got it," Sarah smiles and says "with whom am I speaking with?" Sarah smiles and says.

"It's me, Sarah, Larry."

"Mr, Nicols from PEI vacation?"

"Yes, that's me! Sarah smiles brightly.

"I didn't recognize your voice, how have you been?"

"Great," replies Mr. Nicols. All of a sudden another voice comes on the line.

"Hi, Sarah. I received your last letter on January 12th. I've been busy with school, I haven't had a chance to write you back yet. How are you?"

"Fine, Jeff, thank you."

"It's so great to hear from you guys,"

"Sarah dad is getting antsy so I'll put him back on."

"Ok," says Sarah.

"It's so nice to hear from you Mr. Nicols, what are you up to?"

"Sarah, I'm clutching at straws here."

"Clutching at straws?" asks Sarah.

"Yes, clutching at straws," says Mr. Nicols.

"Do you follow hockey at all?" asks Mr. Nicols.

"Well I watch a little here and there, but that's dad's and my brother David's pastime, they stay more updated on it than I do."

"Well the Maple Leafs are having the second worst season in the last ten year span. And so statistically it looks like it's gonna shape up to be our eighth worst season over all. Ever since the team's beginning."

"Oh, I'm so sorry to hear that," says Sarah."
"But that's why I'm calling," replies Larry. "Our defense is pretty good. Our goalie is well, so, so. And our wingers and centerman just aren't getting very many goals.
"I'm so sorry," replies Sarah.
"Oh, thanks," says Mr. Nichols.
"Well do you remember on vacation you told me about your brother David, and his original shot?"
"Yes says, Sarah."
"I believe you called it a swirl shot," says Mr. Nicols.
"Yes that's it," says Sarah.
"Well that's what I feel the Leafs are missing, an original way to play and execute the game. Sarah I am desperate. As head scout for the Maple Leafs, we got to get the franchise moving. Moving in a better positive direction!!! If I am catching the 11:45 am flight from Air Canada in Toronto to Fredericton, New Brunswick. I have a car waiting for me at the car rental at the airport. And they're leaving a map of New Brunswick on the dash for me. If it's 3pm Atlantic time when the plane lands, how long of a drive is your town from Fredericton? 1 hour and 15 mins," replies Sarah.
"I could be there for 5 pm easily. Would the boys be at the pond at 5pm?"
"Oh, yes, Sarah," replies. "Supper isn't at our house until 6pm. And mom or dad or myself usually have to go up to scrounge out David for supper. But Mr. Nicols, two questions. If you're coming all this way, would you like to have supper with us?"
"I would be honoured," replies Mr. Nicols.
"And my second question is, are you really serious about prospects for the Toronto Maple Leafs?"
"Serious? Serious? A loud voice asks over the phone. We are desperate. If this kid is half as good as you say, not only will we give him a shot! I'll offer him a two year contract to start!!!"
"Wow!!! That's amazing!!!" replies Sarah.
"Well Mr. Nicols, when are you coming?"
"A week from tomorrow Sarah, on February 22nd. And Sarah your brother is in grade twelve, correct?"
"Yes sir, he graduates on June 15th of this year."

Miracle From First Pit Pond

"Well if he is half as good as your friend Emma told me, I'll sign him. Ok, Sarah I have to run, I'm also looking at a kid from Concord, New Hampshire. So I gotta run, I will see you soon. Here is Jeff."
"Ok, bye, bye," replies Sarah.
"Hi Sarah!!" Jeff joyfully says.
"Hello, hello," says Sarah.
"Pretty exciting Ay?" Jeff says.
"Yes it is," says Sarah "but I don't know," says Sarah. "They're just kids on a pond."
"Well they're more than just kids on a pond," says Jeff.
"Remember last summer, Emma said he was really good."
"Yes Jeff, but we are talking about the National Hockey League here."
"Bobby Orr, Doug Gilmore, Billy Smith, Bobby Hull, Rocket Richard. A lot of them came from big cities."
"Sarah, you know the last two players you named?"
"Yes," replies Sarah. Well Rocket Richard and Bobby Hull got their starts on frozen ponds."
"Really? Neat!!!" Says Sarah.
"Did you know Bobby Hill's dad used to get so mad at him because Bobby was a good guy and always did his chores but not until pond hockey was done? Why one time he even took six hay square bundles to the pond on a cold winter's evening so that the pond's fans could have a soft warm place to sit. Bobby's dad came and said "Bobby, the cows are hungry out in the fields. What are you doing?" Bobby smiled and said "playing hockey dad." He was only thirteen years old at the time. He said no one has twenty two cattle hungry out in the fields, almost out of hay. Bobby smiled and said well we have fourteen fans here tonight and I didn't want their butts to get cold!!!"
"Ha, ha, ha," laughed Sarah. "That is funny, is that story true?" Sarah laughs and asks.
Jeff replies and giggles "yes my friend, every word. I read it in the book: *The 50 Craziest Antics of NHL Players before they were NHL.* And where dad has now been promoted to head scout, I get to go on a lot of cool functions with him. I seen Bobby at an NHL gala to raise money for heart disease and I smiled and asked him if

that story was true. He patted me on the shoulder, winked at me and said "every word, young man, every word."

"Ha, ha, ha, ha, ha, that's funny," Sarah replies and laughs.

"I figured a nice maritime farm girl like you would enjoy that story."

"I sure did," says Sarah.

"Well I gotta go finish my chores," says Jeff.

"I gotta wash the supper dishes then I'm done."

"Bye, bye Sarah. I'll write you soon."

"God bless you, Jeff,"

"You too, Sarah," Jeff replies. Sarah hangs up the phone and looks at her mom and smiles. "Mom you know how you look at all your children and encourage us to work hard and believe in our dreams?"

"Yes," Donna June replies as she smiles at Sarah

"Well do you remember I told you about meeting a nice man, Larry Nicols and his son Jeff? On our PEI trip last summer?"

"Yes I do," says Donna June. She takes the tea and tea tray and lays it on the dining room table where they were making their pies.

"Well mom, you're not gonna believe it, but Mr. Nicols is coming down here a week from tomorrow to prospect David."

"What?" shouts out Donna June very loudly. "That's amazing sweetheart," replies Donna June.

"And mom, that's not the half of it. Mr. Nicols said if he is half as good as Emma Melanson told him he was, he is going to sign him to a two year contract with the Toronto Maple Leafs."

"Oh my goodness, oh my goodness!!!" shouts out Donna June. She grabs Sarah and hugs her! "Hunny I have a feeling he's gonna get signed."

"Really mom, you think so?" Asks Sarah.

"Yes, yes, yes!!!" says Donna June. "He is really good," replies Donna June. "I have always raised you kids to be strong, respectful and to never give up!!! I see it in all my children, but I really see it in David. You know all you kids were fully walking by thirteen months old. If I remember correctly, Joseph even was at twelve months. But David, David would always take four or five steps and fall!! Now we all know falling is part of the learning process, but he would never try to fall bum first like most toddlers do. He would always fall face first. But somehow he always seemed to get his hands out in front of him to break his fall."

"Wow Mom, I never knew that about David," replies Sarah."

"Yes, and one time your dad had him in the barn on a warm spring day. He had only been walking about two weeks pointing to the horses, and saying to him "horsies, horsies." Well he heard the door creek open and he looked away for a moment for he thought it was the wind at the door causing it to open, but it was me. "Hi hunny," your dad said to me. "David let go of your dad's leg that he was holding and took steps over to me. I smiled and put my hands out and said, "hi baby boy". Well he tried so fast that the fifth or sixth step he went down face first and never got his hands in front of him to break his fall. Well, luckily there was a lot of hay and straw on the floor, but where his chin hit, his cute little chin with his dimple."

Sarah laughed, "I know mom. He still has that cute little dimple."

"Well it hit and the one little area it hit, it scraped his little chin. For there wasn't any hay or straw in that area. Well your dad and I felt horrible. I ran over and grabbed him and pulled him to me, and hugged him to comfort him. For he was crying pretty loud right?

"Uhhhuh," replied Sarah.

"Well he kept pushing away from me with his arms. I was bouncing him up and down whispering in his ear saying "there, there son, it's okay." But he kept crying and pushing me away. Well your dad came right over and took him because that was what your dad and I both thought he wanted, to be comforted by your dad, but he started to cry even the louder and kept pushing himself away from him. Well Michael held him tight to his chest and sat down on the old barn floor and instantly David stopped crying. He put his hands out in front of him and wanted to be let go of. So your dad left him go. David put his hands out in front of him and took about twelve or thirteen steps.

"Ok," Sarah replied as she listened intently to her mom.

"I smiled and said, "good job baby boy". He looked up and smiled. I put my hands out for him to come, but he turned and walked out hands first right over to your dad. Your dad smiled and said "Good job, son!!!" Put his hands out to take him but David just smiled and turned and walked back to me."

"Wow, that's amazing," said Sarah.

"Well he did that about four or five more times and your dad and I just stood there and watched in amazement. Then the very last time he walked past me, he pushed open the man door in the barn, walked back to the house with his hands out in front of him the whole way. Now of course your dad and I was only four or five feet behind him."

"Did he fall again?" asks Sarah.

"No, not that day," replied Donna June. "But he did a few more times after that, but he always had his hands out in front of him."

"Wow, truly amazing," says Sarah.

Donna June smiles and says "yes, hunny, your dad and I layed in bed that night and talked. We both knew David was special." She paused and looked at Sarah. Donna June walked over to her daughter, put one hand on her shoulder, and another hand on the top right side of her head, and brushed her beautiful long chestnut hair with her hand. "Yes, Sarah, your dad and I knew David was special, but all of our children are special!!!"

"Awwww, mom!!!!" replies Sarah. "I love you very much," says Sarah to her mother.

"I love you very much, too, sweetheart!!!" says Donna June!!"

"Well let's drink our tea before it gets cold."

"Great idea mom," replies Sarah.

As Donna June gives Sarah her cup of tea, and then grabs hers, she just smiles and says "Sarah, I can't believe it, I just can't believe it!!! David is gonna play for the NHL!!!"

"Yes, mame," Sarah smiles and says "the Toronto Maple Leafs!!!!"

If you could have contained all the love in that dining room of that farm house that day, it would have melted the cold -17C snow in the yard. The Gallaghers had grit. The Gallaghers had heart!! The Gallaghers had determination.!! But most importantly, the Gallaghers had love!!!

Chapter 9: And with the Stroke of a Pen, Destiny Begins

"Fight 4320 Air Canada from Toronto to Fredericton is now getting ready to land. Current weather in Fredericton is -19C. Winds are blowing at 7km per hour out of the Northeast. Please make sure your tray tables are put in an upright position and locked. Please be aware that your overhead compartment items could have shifted during flight. Be careful when you open the door. Please make sure your seat is in the upright position, and your seatbelt is fastened. And welcome to Fredericton."
Now of course Larry never heard a word of this because he was sawing about a cord of firewood in his sleep. The stewardess gently shakes him.
"Sir, excuse me sir, sir."
"Huh, huh, what?" Larry mumbles as he is waking up.
"Hi sir, sorry to wake you, but we are getting ready to land in Fredericton. Will you put your chair in the upright position for me please?"
"Yes, no problem, no problem," Larry muttered as he wipes his face with his hands. Larry was under a lot of stress with being promoted to head scout and trying to get the Leafs back into a winning rhythm. But as the plane gets ready to touch down, he smiles, then giggles and thinks to himself. Coming to little ole rural New Brunswick to find the next hot prospect for the Leafs is crazy!!! Crazy but fun!! He thinks back to when he was fifteen and flipped his dirt bike and broke his wrist. Because of popping wheelies!!! That was crazy, but fun!!! He thinks back to the time in college when he and his roommate, Charlie, went to the County Fair and his roommate Charlie betted him $50 that he couldn't

wrestle the prize pig to the ground in under twenty seconds. And how he took the bet and failed miserably. But the on lookers were so impressed that they all threw in their change at him and he made $5.98. Now that was crazy, but fun. And the time that he and his son Jeff went to Ohio for a new prospect for the Leafs. Larry got on a roller coaster. Jeff warned him not to get on it! Larry survived the ride, but he was sick to his stomach, for about three minutes. Over by the bushes as he soon as he got off of Wild Willie!! That was the name of the ride. But it was crazy!! And fun!! So that's how he was looking at this scouting prospect, crazy, but fun!
As they disembarked the plane, Larry was in the very back seat. As he got off the plane and made his way across the tarmac, he walked in the airport and made his way to the rental car booth.
"Hello," a friendly agent said.
"Hello, good afternoon," said Larry.
"My name is Larry Nicols. I have a car reserved for pick up."
"Yes, here is your request, Mr. Nicols, we have you reserved under a mid size car, is that correct?"
"Yes, replied, Larry."
"I have Chevrolets and Fords available today. Do you have any preference, sir?"
"No it doesn't matter," Larry replies.
"Well here is a two year old Ford it only has 17000 km on it, it will work out nicely for you!!!"
"Yes that will be fine," replies Larry.
"Are you here for business or pleasure?" asks the rental agent.
"Business," replies Larry.
"Well, welcome to New Brunswick," replies the friendly young rental agent."
"Thanks, a lot," Larry smiles and says. Larry signs all the paperwork for the credit card and car rental.
"Thank you," says the young rental agent. "If you wanna have a seat in the hallway, I'll have another agent warm it up and bring it right over to you."
"Ok, great," Larry smiles and says.
"Is there anything else I can do for you?" asks the rental agent.

Miracle From First Pit Pond

"Yes," replied Larry. "Can you tell me how far it is to St. Croix, New Brunswick from here?"
"Oh, yes," says the travel agent. "I go out and canoe the river every Summer. It's a clear day the roads are all plowed good. From here under those conditions you're looking at about an hour and twenty minutes from the airport here."
Larry smiles, "Thanks, thanks a lot."
As Larry pulled away in his rental car, his mind began to ponder about many things.

Maybe this would be one big adventure. And besides it seemed everything else the Leafs tried didn't work. So maybe this kid from a little rinky dinky place in New Brunswick could actually lead the Leafs to Stanley Cup glory once again!! As he drove out of Fredericton and into the country, he looked all around at the beauty of this place. The hardwood trees with a layer of snow on the branches. The pines, spruce and firs with their beautiful evergreen branches. Hanging low with the weight of the heavy snow leaning on them. It seemed like no time at all and he was in the outskirts of a quaint little town. As he drove by the sign that said "Welcome to Harvey Station, New Brunswick." He slowed his car down as he wentdown the steep hill into the village. WWE Smith's Country Store came into view. Larry thought to himself a bottle of Sussex Golden Ginger Ale exclusive to the Maritimes would go down good about now.

As Larry parked the car and walked into the store, a pretty young lady working the cash greeted him with a friendly Maritime, "Hello."
"Hi, how are you?" Larry replied.
"Can you tell me how far away I am from St. Croix," Larry asks."
"I sure can," the friendly girl replies."
"It's about a forty minute drive right up the road here. You will drive for about a half an hour then you will come to a town a little bit bigger than ours called McAdam. Stay right on the main road that you came into McAdam on. Go right through town and once you get on the outskirts on the other end on the right up a small hill you will see a large graveyard. Drive right past it then drive

exactly six miles or exactly ten kilometers come to the crossroads then you're in the heart of St. Croix.
"Where are you going in St. Croix?"
"To David Gallagher's," Larry replied.
"I know David. He stops into the store here once in a while when he is on his way to Fredericton. He is a nice guy," she smiles and says!!
"Why, thank you," Larry smiles and says!
He looks in the cooler off to the right and grabs a 500ml bottle of sussex ginger ale, and sets it on the counter. "Will that be all?" the young lady asks.
"Yep," Larry replies.
"That's $1.15 please." Larry lays a two dollar bill on the counter and says "keep the change."
"Thank you," says the young lady. "God bless you and drive safe," she smiles and says.
"Thank you," Larry replies as he grabs his Sussex ginger ale, "God bless you too!!!"

Well Larry thinks to himself, "if I can't land the Leafs their next hot prospect it was worth the trip alone just for the Maritime hospitality and friendliness!!" As he drove through the quaint quiet New Brunswick countryside, he pondered many things. Could a kid from such a tiny little rural community really be the next big thing? Then Larry's mind goes back to the wisdom of his grandpa. Out of the tiniest of seeds, grows the mightiest of trees. And he thought to himself if this kid was even two thirds as good as they say, then David Gallagher may be able to give the Leafs the moral boost they need to start winning more hockey games!! Then he thought of his family and said a quick little prayer. "Lord, thank you for my children and please watch over them until I get home. In Jesus' name, Amen." As he rounded a small turn, he sees a big sign "McAdam Welcomes You." "Only a few more miles to go now!" Larry thought. Larry drove right through town then he saw the headstones up on the hill. "Yep I'm on the right track," he thought. The clock on the dashboard of his rental car said 5:02 pm.

Miracle From First Pit Pond

He should be at the crossroads in St. Croix in six or seven minutes. So the 5:15pm meeting time for Sarah will work out nicely.

As Sarah looked up from her mom's dining room table, she noticed the clock on the wall at 5:03 pm. She would go out and start the car, let it warm up for five or six minutes. Then the three minute drive to the crossroads with her mom, she thought, "we will be three or four minutes early for our meeting with Mr. Nicols". So everything was working out fine Sarah threw her boots on quickly, grabbed the car keys off the keychain holder and started the family car. As she walked back into the farmhouse, she hollered to her mom.
"Mom I got the car started and warming up, it's almost time to drive up to the crossroads to meet Mr. Nicols."
"Oh, ok, thanks sweetheart," she smiled and said as she walked into the kitchen. "
"I can't believe this is really happening mom," Sarah smiles and says!! "An NHL scout for the Toronto Maple Leafs is coming to see David play on First Pit Pond. Can you believe it?"
"Well Sarah, yes, I can actually," Donna June replies as she puts on her heavy winter coat. "You see, sweetheart, ever since David was four years old, even before he was enrolled in Kindergarten, David ate, slept and breathed hockey. He has a true genuine love and passion for it!!! I have always taught all my children, believe in your dreams, follow your dreams, and always give it all you got!!! And David has and did and still does! And hunny, don't forget what the Bible says " If you have faith as big as a grain of mustard seed, you shall say to this mountain, what sweetheart?" Donna June asks Sarah ?"Sarah smiles, "be thou removed."
"Amen!!!" Donna June smiles and says. "Well we better get up to meet Mr. Nicols," Donna June says.
"Yes, mom, lets go." Sarah grabs her coat and walks out the door with her mom. As they pulled out of the driveway, Mr. Nicols was coming to the first of the two cross roads in St. Croix. "Ok, sign says Canterbury, New Brunswick to the right. Saint Stephen, New Brunswick to the left, USA border one mile straight ahead. Yep this has to be the place," he thought to himself. "Oh look here is a wide spot all plowed out nicely and it's nice and level. I'll pull into

here." He pulled in and shut his rental car off. He glanced down at his watch , 5:12pm. "Good I'm three minutes early. I'm sure Sarah will be here soon!!!" As he looks back up out his window, he sees a glance of headlights coming from around the corner. As Donna June's headlights shine on Mr. Nicols rental car, she says to Sarah " that must be Mr. Nicols parked at the wide spot." As Donna June pulled her station wagon along his rental car, he looked over and smiled. Sarah veered ahead of her mom and smiled and waved at Mr. Nicols.

"Yep, that's him mom," Sarah smiled and said.

"Hi, Mr. Nicols," said Sarah!

"Hi Sarah how are you doing?" Mr. Nicols opens his door gently and stands between the two cars. As Donna June exits her door, he sticks out his head and smiles. "Mrs. Gallagher, I presume?" Donna June sticks out her hand and shakes Mr, Nicols hand. "Yes Donna, Donna June Gallagher."

"I'm, Larry, Larry Nicols, head scout for the Toronto Maple Leafs."

Donna June says, "it's a pleasure to meet you Mr. Nicols."

"Please call me Larry."

"Well thank you for coming all the way from Toronto to see David, Larry."

"Mrs. Gallagher, let me ask you a question," Larry says. "How good would you say your son Daivd is?"

"Very, very, very, good I'd say, Larry," Donna June replied. "You drive with us to First Pit Pond, and you will see for yourself."

"Well Mrs. Gallagher in the NHL we have what are called enforcers. Every NHL team has them. If he can't be versatile, agile and fast then they will chew him up and spit him out and keep on trucking and not even bat an eye.

"Mr. Nicols come over here for a minute with me please." Donna June walks to the back of her station wagon. Donna June opened up the back of her station wagon.

"Mr. Nicols," she says "as she hands him a baseball bat, what is this?"

Miracle From First Pit Pond

"A baseball bat," he says. "True," replied Donna June. That's a Louisville slugger made in Louisville, Kentucky, USA."

"It's a very fine product," Donna June says.

"It's made of quality hickory wood from the Kentucky hollers. Mrs. Gallagher, I'm here for hockey not baseball," replies Larry.

"Hold on, I'm not done," Donna June replies. She pulls out a box of twenty two rifle shells, opens the box and pulls out a bullet. "Mr. Nicols, do you know what this is?" Larry takes it out of her hand, examines it and replies, "I assume that it is a bullet of some sort."

Donna June smiles and says, "correct."

"This will kill a rabbit at forty five yards. It will stop a coyote, dead in his tracks with a head shot up to thirty four yards. And this bullet will bring down a 6'5'' 295 lbs man or a 5'6'' 158 lbs man or any size between dead in their tracks at twenty four yards."

Larry chuckles and looks up at Donna June.

"Mrs. Galagher, do you moonlight as an enforcer for the mob?" He asks.

"No, I don't," Donna June says. " I have these items in my car, for probably reasons you would never think of."

"Ok," asks Mr. Nicols, "why do you have these items in your car?" Donna June replies, "a lot of the time when the cattle are out grazing, if you pick up a bat, and hit rocks with it, the sound is usually enough to get them to listen to my common, and rustle them into the barn. But if that does not work, if I shout HEY MOVE three times very loudly, and shoot this one bullet out of the gun into the ground twenty feet away in a safe location, they obey every word I say and they get to the barn, and get going fast."

"Mrs. Gallagher, what exactly are you trying to tell me here?" asks Larry.

"I grew up in the city, I don't know much about farming," replied Larry. Donna June smiled and replied, "well Mr. Nicols I'm trying to give you an illustration of how small can be very, very, effective!! My son David may not be the largest guy, but he's tough as whale bone and he can move, skate, stop, rotate. But I must say he is more like this bullet than the bat."

"Not quite sure I'm following, Mrs. Gallagher," replied Larry.

"Well let's say you were walking down a street in Toronto very late at night. And a guy approached you almost twice your size with this bat, and said to you, "I want all your money, and I want it now." Not a good situation wouldn't you agree?" asks Donna June.
"Absolutely," Larry says. "But if I said I don't think so and pull this one twenty two caliber rifle bullet out of your pocket, unless you can get the bat out away from him, you are probably toast!!"
"Yes, I'd say so!" replied Larry.
"But if in your hand was that same bullet inside the gun cocked loaded and the safety button off, we now have a totally different scenario, don't we?"
"Yes, I'd say so," replied Larry.
"So are you trying to tell me David is the bullet, and gun and all in the chambers, locked and loaded and ready?" Donna June smiled.
"No, Larry what I'm trying to tell you is that bat is strong. Made with fine quality Kentucky hickory wood. But it will break at a force of 173 psi pressure when swung. And it only swings as fast as the man swinging it. This bullet leaves the end of the gun barrel at fourteen hundred feet per second. And the first five hundred yards it hits with over 23,000 psi, then slowly decreases."
"So you think he can go up against the enforcers and win?" asks Larry.
"No," Mr. Nicols," replies Donna June.
"He eats, sleeps and breathes hockey."
"The southeast side of our barn. We have a three foot by six inch section that has to be replaced every August."
"Why's that?" asks Mr. Nicols.
Donna June replies "because he fires so many hockey pucks against that section of the barn. Well that, he literally beats it to pieces. If a cow was to lean against it, it is weakened enough it would bust right open."
"Every August?" Larry asks. "Every August."
"Maybe you shouldn't use a half an inch of plywood for your repairs, maybe you should use three quarter an inch."
"We use maple boards," replies Donna June.
"One inch maple boards?" Larry asks as his eyes bug out!!"
"That's a hardwood yes," says Donna June.

Miracle From First Pit Pond

"He literally hits it so much it weakens it that bad?"
"Yes," says Donna June.
"Wow, that's amazing!" replies Larry.
"You see, he plays on the pond. They are always on it by Christmas time if not before. But after March 10th or 11th when it isn't safe to be on, he practices his shooting in the barn. But why not a bigger section of the wall why only three feet by six inches."
"Because, Mr. Nicols, he's so good, that's the only spot he hits."
"Impressive," says Larry. "From twenty feet?" he asks.
"No," says Donna June, "the width of our barn is forty four feet, it runs southwest to southeast and the length of it is fifty six feet and it runs northwest to southwest. He stands against the southwest wall when he lets it rip," replies Donna. "But I say all that to say all this, at the age of nine, he developed those skills, and has been doing it ever since."
"Wow!!!" replies Mr. Nicols. Mr. Nicols smiles and asks Donna June a question.
"So I guess what you're saying is he is like the bullet, but after it is fired out of the barrel of the gun?"
"That's exactly what I'm saying Mr. Nicols," Donna June replies. "Louisville slugger bats are big and strong, and will hurt you if you are hit with one. But a bullet is small, but it will drop you everytime!"
"Well if all this is true," replies Mr. Nicols, "I'll guarantee him a try out with the Leafs!!"
"Oh, it's true, Mr. Nicols," replies Sarah. "Every single word of it!!"
Donna June puts the bullet and bat away. Mr. Nicols says to Donna June, "Well Mrs. Gallagher, I can't wait to see your son in action!!!"
"Mr. Nicols, there is one more thing you should be aware of."
"What is that?" he asks Donna June.
"I've raised all my children to have strength and tenacity to never ever give up!! This is a skill that you might find appealing as well!!! And out of all my children, I can honestly tell you, David is one of the strongest!"
"Well I can't wait to see him in action!!" Replies Mr. Nicols.

"Mr. Nicols there is also one more thing you should know about, two actually," says Saraah
"What would that be?" Asks Mr. Nicols.
"Well the first is, I've never met anyone with such a love for hockey as David. And I mean no one," says Sarah.
"Okay," replies Larry. "And the second thing Sarah?"
"Well my class has already decided we are gonna raise money and go on a class trip to Boston in grade ten. So you better look at him while you can. You never know, I could run into a scout down there for the Bruins. Mr. Nicols chuckles, "Now we wouldn't want that would we?" he asks Sarah. They all laugh!
"No we wouldn't," replies Donna June.
"Mrs. Gallagher, it was a pleasure to meet you!! Sarah nice to see you as always!! Now get me to this New Brunswick pond as soon as possible please!" Mr. Nicols jumps into his red rental car and fires it up. "Follow Sarah and I, shouts out Donna June."
"That was a great analogy back there, mom," says Sarah as Donna June pulls out onto the road and heads for First Pit Pond!"
"Thanks, sweetheart," replies Donna June. "It reminded me of David and Goliath, in the Bible. Goliath was more than twice the size of David, but with one smooth stone, he was brought down. Don't forget the most important part of that beautiful Bible story," says Donna June.
"What's that mama?"
"You came to me with a sword and shield, but I come to you in the name of the Lord. He will deliver you unto me this day. The rock wasn't the only thing that brought Goliath down. God was there too.
"And you know what mama?" replies Sarah.
"What sweetheart?"
"With man this is impossible, but with God all things are possible."
"Amen, sweetheart, Amen!!"

At First Pit Pond, David slams one in, but Stephen Therialt blocks it quickly with his left leg pad. Stephen is covered with icy slush where as David's skates are razor sharp as he skids to a quick stop.

"See Stephen, you're getting better!! Like I told you, when you see me start to raise my stick, let your legs relax a little. That way, eyes on the shooter, but reflexes are loosening for your legs to move quickly."

"Thanks, David." Stephen smiles and says. LeRoy Gardner skates over and says "Hey David, what are you gonna do? Coach for the Vancouver Canucks?"

"Yea, maybe," David smiles and says, "after I play a few years for the Toronto Maple Leafs first."

"Ha, ha, ha, ha," laughs LeRoy "like I said, as if that's gonna happen."

"Hey guys, who's that coming in the shiny car behind David's mom?" Asks Darrell Cairns.

"I don't know," says Stephen, but that's a nice looking car. As Larry parks his car on the side of the road, and walks towards the pond, LeRoy Gardner shouts out, "Hey Mr, who are you?"

Mr. Nicols smiles and says, "Hi, I'm looking for David, David Gallagher."

"What do you want him for?" asks LeRoy. See LeRoy might have been a little rough around the edges, but he truly loved and cared for David. Almost like a little brother.

"Well I'm LeRoy, LeRoy Garnder," Mr. Nicols smiles and extends his hand. "Hi, nice to meet ya," as LeRoy shakes his hand, Larry says,goodstronggripthereyoungman. "ya cutting and splitting wood for years will do that to ya." Larry applies a little strength into his grip. LeRoy replies, "not a bad grip either there Mr? "I'm Mr. Larry Nicols, nice to meet ya."

"Nice to meet you I'm LeRoy, LeRoy Gardner." At this time Saraha and Donna June have exited their car and walked over to the pond.

"Stocking shelves on the graveyard shift for eight hours in college will give ya a pretty good grip too," replies Larry.

"So what are ya doing here?" Asks LeRoy again.

"Well as I said I'm Larry Nicols, head scout for the Toronto Maple Leafs and I'm looking for David Gallagher. Is he here this evening?"

"Toronto Maple Leafs?" asks Darrell Cairns. "Like the NHL Toronto Maple Leafs?"

"That's right," Larry smiles and says. LeRoy's jaw drops. David immediately skates over to the edge of the pond. He begins to hurriedly wave Sarah and Donna June over. As Sarah walks over to her brother, she immediately sees his big ol crocodile tears rolling down his face. Sarah just smiles and says, "yes big brother!!!!!" David just grabs her and hugs her, and begins to cry some more.
"I love you Sarah!!! I love you Sarah!!! I love you Sarah!!!" David repeats as he hugs her. By this time Donna June is standing there.
"Hi, son!" she smiles and says.
"Hi, mom!" David smiles and says as he hugs her. David grabs a hold of his sister again! Hugs her again, "I love you, Sarah! I can't believe you did this for me!"
"David, I didn't do anything," Sarah smiles and says, " you and Jesus did it!!!" As David looks at his mom he says "oh mom, mom," he says. "I can't believe this and he smiles brightly!!"
"This is your shot David," his mother smiles and says. "We are all very proud of you David," says Donna June. As this is going on, everyone skates over to Mr. Nicols, removes their hockey gloves and begins to introduce themselves. Mr. Nicols smiles as he shakes every one of their hands. Stephen leaves the net and skates over and takes off his goalie helmet and gloves and sticks out his hand.
"Hello, Mr. Nicols, nice to meet you! I'm Stephen, Stephen Theriault." As this is taking place, Donna June places her hand on David's shoulder and says "David, now listen to me."
"Yes, mom," says David.
"Remember I can do all things through Christ who strengthens me Phillippians 4:13, replies David." Donna smiles, now go out there and have fun, do what you do best and remember you're a Gallagher.
As David skates away, Sarah calls out with a loud voice. "Hey David?"
"Yes, little sister," David says.
"Give em hell big brother." David winks and smiles at his sister.
"Sarah!!" Donna June says.
"Awww mom, just once."

"Ok," Donna June smiles and says.
While all this is going on, Stephen turns and points to his good friend David coming across the ice.
"And Mr. Nicols, that's my good friend David Gallagher, Stephen smiles and says." David skates over, removes his helmet and gloves and smiles brightly. "Hi, Mr Nicols. Nice to see you. I'm David, David Gallagher,"
"David, the pleasure is all mine! I'm Larry Nicols, head scout with the Toronto Maple Leafs! I have come here this evening to watch you play some hockey."
"Yes sir!" David smiles and says as he buttons the chin strap of his helmet and puts his gloves on.
"All right everybody, line up," says Mr. Nicols as he blows a whistle.
"Hey Sarah," yells Larry.
"Yes, Mr. Nicols," Sarah replies.
"Will you grab me my pencil and clipboard out of the passenger seat of my car please?"
"Yes, sir," replies Sarah.
Sarah opens his car door, grabs the items, walks them down to Mr. Nicols on the pond. "Thank you Sarah," he says as she hands it to him.
"Ok roll call left to right. "Red sweater kid."
"Brandon Copp sir."
"Alright," says Mr. Nicols. "Number two."
"Marty Gardner, sir."
"Ok, nice Flyers Jersey, by the way. Number three."
"Darrell Cairns."
"Ok," says Mr. Nicols. "Number four."
"Peter Eales, sir."
"Ok Mr. Eales," says Larry. "Number five."
"LeRoy Gardener, sir."
"LeRoy I really like your old bauers."
"Thank you," says LeRoy. "They were my dad's."
"Nice kid, nice," replies Larry. "Number six."
"Stephen Theriault, sir."
"Thank you, Stephen," replies Mr. Nicols. "Number seven."
"And I'm David, David Gallagher." David says proudly.

"Ok, Davey boy," replies Larry.

Mr. Nicols takes off his hat, scratches his head, chuckles and puts his hat back on his head. "Ok we got seven guys," replies Larry. "But how do ya's play with only one goalie?"

"Oh, that's easy," replies Peter Eales.

"It is?" asks Larry.

"Yes, our team's are three on three, Stephen is the goalie for both sides."

"Oh, okay, I see," replies Larry. "Ok guys I'd like these three guys to go to one edge of the pond please, Peter Eales, Darrell Cairns, and LeRoy Gardner. Ok, David Galagher, Brandon Copp and Marty Gardner to the center of the pond please. Stephen Theriault take your net now please."

"Yes, sir, Mr. Nicols," replies Stephen.

"Ok, guys this is a three on three, anyone here wear glasses?"

"I do, to read," says LeRoy Gardner to Mr. Nicols.

"Ok, kid, no problem," says Larry. "How about you David?" asks Mr. Nicols.

"No, sir," David replies. Mr. Nicols reaches into his coat and pulls out of his pocket two red spools of thread. He looks all around the pond, walks over around four feet from the shore, he places thread there. "Ok, guys on the opposing team of David, I want you guys to do everything you can to distract David, and to stop David from getting off a shot! Do not let him shoot if possible, ok?"

"Ok, sir," replies Darrell Cairns to Mr. Nicols.

"Now these two spools of rolled out red thread are the presuming center line. David try not to go outside past the center line ok?"

"Ok, sir," replies David. Mr. Nicols goes to roughly the centre of the pond. Marty Gardner faces off against Peter Eales. Mr. Nicols smiles "ok, ready guys?"

"Yep," the boys reply.

Larry blows his whistle, smiles and says "let's play some hockey," and drops the puck. Peter wins the face off and quickly passes it to LeRoy, who heads towards the center line. David outskates him and quickly takes the puck as LeRoy lifts his stick to clear it. David turns quick as a cat and approaches the net, quickly firing a shot on Stephen from roughly two feet out. Stephen barely clears it

Miracle From First Pit Pond

with his stick. Larry watches very intently. Larry blows his whistle quickly. "Nice boys, nice," he says "great hustle everyone." As Larry walks to the red threads, representing the center line, "David come over here please."

"Yes, Mr. Nicols," David says as he skates over.

"I want you to stand four feet from this thread centerline, ok?"

"Ok, sir," David replies.

"David, by a free hand shot, do you think you could hit Stephen's chest or shoulders?"

"From here?" says David.

"Yes, right from where I am standing."

"Sure, no problem," replies David.

"LeRoy, will you come here please?"

"Sure, sir."

Larry reaches into his other pocket. "LeRoy skate to the end of this measuring tape to Stephen's sternum on his chest."

"Ok, sir." LeRoy quickly skates down, "ok, sir." Larry measures it, seventy three feet, nine inches.

"David, did you realize it was that far?"

"Naa," replies Stephen, we have never taken any measurements here."

"Do you still think from here you can hit his chest or shoulders?"

"Sure, no problem," replies David.

Larry looks pondered, "David I don't think you can," replies Larry.

"Umm…. Mr. Nicols from here, I can hit his center of his chest, the right side of his chest, or one right shoulder. The left side of his chest or left shoulder."

Mr. Nicols takes his hat off again, runs his hand through his hair, looks at David and grins. "Ok, young man, let's see what you got." Donna June and Sarah are leaning against the fender of the station wagon watching. Larry drops three pucks roughly seven feet apart. "Ok, kid, once you hit the center of his chest, skate towards him, turn, reposition, then hit his left side. Same thing, turn, reposition, then hit his right side."

"Ok, no problem," replies David.

Larry blows the whistle, Stephen goes to the center puck slap shots it in, it hits Stephen about three inches above his sternum. He skates about a third of the way down, comes back, stops, looks for one split second, fires the puck to the right, and hits Stephen almost perfectly center of his left shoulder socket. He skates out about ten feet, turns, looks quickly and slaps the final one in, hitting Stephen between his right shoulder and right breast on his chest.

"Wow, I can't believe what I'm seeing," Larry says to himself. Larry blows his whistle, "ok boys, everybody please come over to me one more time. The teams are now everybody on the ice against David."

"What!" says LeRoy.

"Yep, David tries to score goals, everyone else tries to stop him. David, go near center line thread. Darrell and LeRoy skate back to Stephen where they are the biggest." Larry kicks a puck over to David, blows his whistle, "let's go."

Peter quickly approaches David and makes a grab for the puck, but David quickly skates around him, Brandon and Marty are coming on to him, he gets by Brandon, but shoves Marty for control of the puck. Marty loses balance and falls over. He approaches LeRoy turns last minute. Fires on in, Stephen almost gets it with a quick glove save, but it just got by last minute. Larry blows the whistle, "nicely done everyone." Larry drops another one near the center thread. Blows his whistle, David skates down Brandon checks him, David stumbles but gets around him. Peter and Marty pursue the chase,but cannot keep up to David. As he approaches the left hand side, David sees Darrell approaching. Darrell checks him hard, but David rushes behind net fast where the puck is. LeRoy checks him again. Darrell falls flat on his buttocks, but manages to make a sweeping shot around Stephen, falling on the puck just in time. Larry blows the whistle. "Well I've seen all I need to see," replies Larry. "David will you please come here quickly?"

David gets to his feet and gets face to face with Stephen. Ready to have an NHL goalie tryout shot pal?" David asks Stephen.

"David, what are you doing?" Stephen says with a confused look as he slips off his helmet.

"What do you mean what am I doing? This is a shot for you, a shot of a lifetime!! For a NHL Canadian team!"

Miracle From First Pit Pond

"If I keep working and practicing hard, maybe other shots will come along."

"But I'll only have one best friend, and that's you Stephen," David smiles and says.

"Awww, David, that means a lot to me coming from you, but you go for it, this is your dream buddy!!"

"Stephen, let me ask you a question!"

"Ok," Stephen smiles and says.

"My question is you have been listening and applying what I have been teaching you, correct?"

"Yes, that is correct," Stephen answers.

"Well would you turn down a chance to play pro hockey if it was offered to you?"

"No, I wouldn't turn it down," says Stephen, "it would be amazing!!!"

"Well keep listening to me and keep applying what I have been teaching you!" David winks and says "besides it isn't any worse then what they have now!" Both boys chuckle.

"So what do you say Stephen?

"Let's do this!"

"Ok," Stephen smiles and says.

David rushes over to Mr. Nicols.

"Mr. Nicols?"

"Yes, young man," replies Larry.

"I'd love to have a tryout with the Toronto Maple Leafs."

"Well that's just great," replies Larry.

"But I'll only come try out on one condition," says David.

"What?" screams Darrell Cairns.

"What, are you crazy?" shouts LeRoy Gardner.

"Well what is your condition, David? Asks Larry.

David smiles and raises his stick at Stephen. Stephen takes a stance in his net. David breaks away skates eight or ten feet and lets a slapshot go for the net. Stephen relaxes his legs, uses his stick as a blocker, and falls to his knees. Stephen stands up after blocking the shot and hits the puck away back towards Mr. Nicols. The condition is that Stephen goes with me as well Mr. Nicols and he gets a try out too." Larry takes his hat off and scratches his head.

LeRoy skates over and says, "Mr. Nicols give me a second here with David, please."
"Sure, LeRoy," replies Larry.
"No problem."
"David, what are you doing?" Asks LeRoy.
"What are you talking about LeRoy?" Asks David.
"Well I think you may have a real shot here. I mean think about it, this guy came the whole way from Toronto just to see you!"
"Ok, and?" Asks David.
"Well I said he came the whole way from Toronto to see you, not Stephen. If I was you, I wouldn't worry about Stephen. I would just concentrate on you."
"Hey, LeRoy, after Stephen you are my oldest friend in the world."
"Ya, and?" asks LeRoy.
"Well just make sure you have a place set for Stephen to, when you personally host the shin dig when we bring the Stanley Cup home to St. Croix one day!!!" LeRoy smiles.
"Go, get em buddy."
Now at that moment in time, I don't know if we all have a destiny or not, but David sure did seem to know and believe he did. To bring the cup home to St. Croix, New Brunswick one day. Mr. Nicols looks around that pond as David is skating over to him, and he thinks to himself "in eleven years of scouting he has never heard or seen anything like this before." David skates over and takes a knee in front of Mr. Nicols.
"Mr. Nicols," says David. "Ever since I was four years old, I wanted to be an NHL player. My family and I would watch hockey night in Canada. I can still remember my dad giggling as I would watch the leafs play the Blackhawks, or Bruins, or Canadians and how I would roar with excitement and jump up and down and try to call plays in my little four year old mind. I can still see my mom yelling as well. "David stop jumping on the couch." David smiles as he recollects these memories. "So you see Mr. Nicols the fact that you would come all the way from Toronto and watch me play on First Pit Pond, well sir, it's amazing!!! It's a dream come true for me actually. But I would have never in my wildest dreams have dreamt that an NHL scout, let alone a head NHL scout for my

favorite team would come to our lil old pond and offer me a try out. But it did, didn't it sir?"
"Yes David, it did," replies Larry. But the offer was extended to you and not to Stephen."
"Mr. Nicols, how do you win hockey games?" asks David.
"Strength, determination, conditioning and grit are all good things wouldn't you say?"
"Yes David," answers Larry. "And I see all that in you."
"What about scoring goals?" asks David.
"Yes, definitely," replies Mr. Nicols.
"But there is one very important point sir, you are forgetting, concerning my question, so I will ask you again. How do you win hockey games?"
"You stop goals as well! Mr. Nicols when I was ten years old, Stephen asked me if I wanted to race. I said race? He said ya. I said sure. No where could we go, where we were just little. We were at my house, so I said let's go to the front of the barn, touch it, and back to the well cover whoever gets here first wins! So Sarah said on your mark, get set, go. Now at the start Stephen was out in front of me by at least a good three to four feet. When we got to the barn, we were neck in neck, going back for about half to two thirds of the way. I was holding tight to him but at the last end Stephen gave it all he had, I tried and tried and tried, but I couldn't even stay with him let alone get out in front of him. He beat me to the well over and touched it by at least twelve or thirteen in front of me. So Stephen clearly won that race fair and square. So later on in life, oh I suppose we were almost fifteen years old. We were tenting out up on Bolton Lake one night fishing and roasting wieners, cooking our fish over an open fire, it was great!!" Larry smiles, "sounds like it was!"
"Oh yea!!" David smiles and says. "Anyway as we were there just roasting wieners, I said hey Stephen remember when we were little kids and you asked me to race and I said sure? Yes I remember replied Stephen. Well I remember that afternoon well you beat me and beat me by at least ten feet. Stephen giggled ya I know David, what about it? Well buddy I said, I thought I could take you and do it quite easily! Hey! Stephen said as he gently poked me in my shoulder. No honestly, I thought I could but you whooped the

pants right off me! Buddy my question is how, how did you. Stephen looked at me very seriously and he said David not to sound rude, but I was confident I'd beat you long before I ever asked. Really? David asks. Yes Stephen smiled and said. But wanna know where that confidence was from? Sure david replies. Well ever since I was four years old Stephen says I never ever walked anywhere. I always ran. I've never seen you run before, said david. Oh around you or with our friends in the arcade Friday nights, I never ran but going to school, coming home from school, going to my uncle's house going down to the store for mom, I always ran. Wow replied David. Stephen smiled, I can run like the wind buddy!"

"Great story," says Mr. Nicols.

"Thank you," says David. "But what I'm trying to convey to you Mr. Nicols is this. By the outer appearance, things aren't always what they appear to be!"

"Interesting!!!" replies Mr. Nicols.

"I'm telling you Mr. Nicols, Stephen has the potential to become an excellent goaltender."

"Do you really think so, David?" Asks Larry.

"Yes, I truly believe it, sir! With all my heart," David smiles and says.

Mr. Nicols looks up into the sky. The daylight is now gone and the stars are out, it's a bright clear winter's night.

"Well you know a goalie with great potential couldn't hurt us any Mr. Nicols!" says David. "In my opinion if you had a remarkable goalie, and a little stronger defensive, in my opinion, the Leafs would be unstoppable!!"

"You know kid, I have been thinking the same thing," says Larry. Larry chuckles,"maybe you should think of becoming a scout instead of a player!!" David smiles and says "well as soon as I win a Stanley Cup or two, I just may!

"Sarah," Larry calls out.

"Yes Mr. Nicols," replies Sarah.

"I assume in a country setting like this, you, Stephen, and David all attend the same school?"

"Yes sir, that's correct," replies Sarah.

"When is your March break?" asks Larry.
"March 5th-11th," replies Sarah..
"sarah in the back seat of my rental car, my briefcase is laying on the seat. Will you grab it and bring it down to me, please?"
"Yes, sir," replies Sarah.
"Thank you!" says Larry. Mr. Nicols pulls out his daily scheduler from his shirt pocket, inside his coat. "Ok, let's see," says Mr. Nicols. "March 5th home against Detroit. March 6th, off. March 7th on the road in Boston. March 8th on the road in Philadelphia. March 10th at home against St. Louis, perfect.
Sarah asks as she's coming with the briefcase, "where would you like it, Mr. Nicols?"
"Just by my feet is good! Thank you so much Sarah."
"You are welcome." Sarah smiles and says.
"David stand to your feet please," says Larry as he bends down and opens up his briefcase. He removes two neatly folded pieces of paper and a pen. As David arises, Mr. Nicols says "Stephen, will you come here please?"
"Yes, sir," replies Stephen. Stephen skates over quickly.
"Stephen how would you feel about watching a game with your friends Peter Eales, Marty Gardner, Brandon Copp, Darrell Cairns, LeRoy Gardner, and David Gallagher?"
"Are you kidding sir, I'd love it," replies Stephen. Stephen joyfully replies well excellent guys!!! The boys break out cheering in unison, they are so happy!!!
"Darrell, will you come here please?"
"Sure," says Darrell.
"You're pretty broad across the back, I may come back next year and gather you for a defenceman!"
"Ha, ha, ha," laughs Darrell. "I'll be here!" Stephen you will unwind nicely with your friends at the game after your official tryout with the Toronto Maple Leafs!!! Mr. Nicols unfolds the official try out paper on Darrell's back. Stephen this is an official try out offer, it's not a guarantee of an offer, but it does guarantee, we fly you out, fly you back, put you up in a motel and feed you and arrange your transportation. So would you like to sign this?
"Oh yes sir," Stephen smiles and says and David, the same for you!"

"Yes, sir," David replies as he signs! And with the stroke of a pen, a destiny begins!!!

Chapter 10: Hockey Sticks, Hugs and Plane Rides

"LeRoy, here is my phone number, can you have all your friends get a permission slip signed by their mom or dad, just a note giving me permission for them to come?"
"Oh, sure Mr. Nicols, replies LeRoy!"
"Great," says Larry. "Once you confirm it, all you call me, I will give you flight numbers and the hotel address and the hotel room numbers ok?"
"Ok, sir," LeRoy smiles and says!
"Oh and we will have a car and driver for your transportation to!"
"Great, thanks," replies LeRoy!!!
"Yea, thanks all the boys tell, Larry."
"David, your friends will be flying out March 8th in the morning. You and Stephen will be flying out the morning of March 6th, Larry makes a note in his scheduler. So Stephen and David do we have a deal?"
"Oh, yes sir," Stephen smiles and says and shakes his hand.
"Yes sir, thank you sir, you are literally making a personal dream of mine come true!"
"You're welcome young man," replies Larry.
"My pleasure," as he shakes David's hand.
"I'll call David with your and his flight details as the day approaches."
"Ok," Stephen.
"Yes, sir, thank you sir," replies Stephen.
"Everyone, it was great to meet you all, and I will see ya's all the evening of March 10th at the gardens," says Larry!
"God bless you all."

"God bless you sir," shouts out Stephen as Larry walks off the pond with his briefcase. The boys talk amongst themselves for a second. Then all of a sudden Leroy hollers out "Hey Mr. Nicols," Larry stops, and turns.
"Yes Leroy?" ready guys, LeRoy asks.
They all shout out in unison, "Thank you!" Mr. Nicols smiles and waves! "You're welcome."
"And our team is called The St. Croix Miracles."
"Ok," says Larry.
"That's right," David says as him and Stephen skates over, beside their friends. "Miracles from First Pit Pond." David smiles and proudly says, as Larry walks up the incline to the road, he looks at Sarah and Donna June!
"Ladies, thanks for everything."
"You're welcome," says Sarah.
Sarah walks down to the pond, puts out her arms and hugs her brother. "I'm proud of you, big brother."
"Aww thanks lil sis," replies David. "I love you!!"
"I love you, too," replies Sarah! "Now remember when you get up there, you show him what us Maritimers are made of!!!"
As Donna June walks onto the pond, Stephen looks at her, brightly and smiles. "Mrs. Gallagher, I can't believe it!" replies Stephen. Mrs. Gallagher gives him a big hug and says, "Stephen, you keep smiling, and doing your best. You don't know what good things God has in store for you!!"
"I will!!" replies Stephen.
Sarah walks off the pond back to Mr. Nicols by his rental car.
"Well Sarah, it was great to see you again!" replies Larry. "Thanks for telling me about your brother, he's quite remarkable!"
"You're welcome," replies Sarah.
"We will come by and visit you folks in August when I'm on vacation."
"That would be just lovely," replies Sarah.
"But mom and I have been talking. It's 6:35 pm now," Sarah says as she looks at her wrist watch.
"When does your flight go back in the morning?" Sarah asks.
"9:00 am," replies Larry.

Miracle From First Pit Pond

donna June walks up to Sarah and Larry, "do you have any plans for supper," asks Donna June?
"Well no actually I don't," replies Larry.
"Oh, man are you in luck," says Sarah. "Mom made one of her homemade peach pies for dessert!"
"No we are all in luck," replies Donna June.
"Sarah made her youth group award winning meatloaf!"
"That all sounds lovely," replied Larry.
All of a sudden, Stephen stands there smiling. "Man you got your skates off and shoes on quick!" replies Larry.
"I guess running and racing aren't the only things you're fast at!" Larry chuckles and says.
"Got room for one more for supper, Mrs. Gallagher?" asks Stephen. Donna June laughs and says, "yes."
"Yes, Stephen, we do, you are more than welcome!! I wouldn't have asked, but it's that pie and meatloaf," Stephen smiles and says! Larry chuckles. "Pretty good stuff, say Stephen?" says Larry.
"Mr. Nicols, do you believe in God?" asks Stephen.
"Well yes, I do,' replies Mr. Nicols. "How about yourself?"
"I never miss a youth service," Stephen smiles and says. "But I gotta tell ya, Mr. Nicols. A little piece of Heaven has come down to earth and it's on the Gallagher kitchen table! And you are gonna have the pleasure of experiencing it in about fifteen minutes."
"Sounds great," replies Larry.
David walks up to the road with hockey gloves on and skates dropped over the end of his hockey stick." He smiles and slaps David on the back. "Come on buddy let's go eat."

Well time never stops ticking and it's late afternoon on March 5th. And David finds himself with a suitcase open on his bed. And Saraha is going over a checklist with him!!! "Ok, brown cotton pants?" asks Sarah. "Check," says David. "Red sweater?" "Check" "Black dress pants?""check". "Blue jeans, two pairs?" "check" "green sweater?" check. "Red tie and one dress shirt white in color?" check. "Three plain black t-shirts?" check. "Okay let's see," says Sarah. "Four pairs of ankle socks? Check "one pair of thick wool socks?" check "four pairs of underwear?" check. "One pair of pajama pants?" check. "One pair of gym pants?" check

"and one pair of hockey skates, sharpened like razors?" check, check. David smiles and says.
"Big brother are you sure you shouldn't pack more socks and underwear?"
"No," replies David. "Mr. Nicols said the hotel he has booked for us has a free laundry service at 10:00am every morning. You just leave a little card on your door. Put your dirty laundry in a plastic laundry bag they provide for you, and leave it on your bed. They pick it up, wash it, dry it, return it, and fold it and place it back on your bed all before 5:00 pm so that it will work out well. "Wow, fancy!!!" Saraha smiles and replies.
THe phone begins to ring beside David' bed. "Want me to get it, big brother?" asks Sarah
Sure," replies David.
"Hello,"
"Hi Saraha, how are you doing?" a kind voice asks over the phone.
"I'm great, and you?"
"Oh, great, i'm just so excited for the big trip tomorrow."
"Awesome, are ya all packed, ready and waiting!!"
"Hey are you and your dad still coming into the Fredericton airport with me, David and my dad?
"Are you kidding? We wouldn't miss it!"
"Ok, I'll see ya at 4:00 am tomorrow bright and early tomorrow, ok Stephen?"
"Sure!!! Is David there, can I talk to him for a minute?"
"Sure, just a sec!"
"David, Stephen wants you on the phone."
"Ok, thanks sis," say's David.
"Hello, Hey buddy how are ya?" asks Stephen.
"Doing great," replies David, "and you"?
"Awesome, man, awesome!" says Stephen.
"We will be at your house at 4:00 am sharp and you and your dad be up and ready ok?"
"Oh, we will!!" says Stephen. Later pal."
"Later," says David.
The next morning Stephen and David anxiously await the check in line. As their turn approaches David says to the agent.

"Hi, my name is David Gallagher and this is my best friend Stephen Theriault. We have two tickets to pick up here."
"Yes, sir," says the pretty young check in lady for the Toronto Maple Leafs, no less!"
"Yes Miss, that's correct." David smiles and says.
"It says that on your computer screen?" David asks. She smiles, "yes, it does," she says. "Are you guys going up for a big game," she asks.
"No, we are going up for a tryout!" replies David.
"Well that's great," replies the check-in agent.
"Thanks," David smiles and says.
"Ok, you guys have a suitcase, a piece to check-in?"
"Yes," replies Stephen. "Ok, just leave them here with me, your suitcases will be at the carousel when you arrive in Toronto. Here are your boarding passes. Have fun, good luck and just turn left to go through security." As a husband and wife get ready to go through security, Sarah reaches over the railing to hug Stephen and Daivd.
"Good luck guys."
"Thank you, Sarah," replies Stephen. Sarah hugs David. "Good luck, big brother."
"Thanks, lil sis," David smiles and says. "I love you very much!"
"I love you too, big brother," says Sarah Stephen and David's dads both smile and wave at the boys! "And remember," says Michael, "you're Maritimers, you are tough stock. Call us when you get checked in guys," says Michael..
"We will," says David. David and Stphen complete their security check, then sit and wait to board the plane. As boarding is complete, they go on the plane and each take their seat.

"It's my first time flying," David smiles and tells Stephen. "Are you nervous?" asks Stephen. "No, not really," says David. "I flew to Florida four years ago with my mom and dad and sister. We went to Disney World."
"Oh, that was nice," says David. "There's nothing to it," replies Stephen. "I'm not nervous about flying, but I am nervous about my tryout with the Leafs," replies David.

"Why?" asks Stephen. "David you will probably get signed after them just watching you for ten minutes. But I'm not as good as you," replies Stephen. David giggles, "they will sign you after watching you for twenty minutes." The boys share a giggle. Stephen smiles and says "buddy let's just give it one hundred and ten percent and see what happens. "Ok,pal," David smiles and says.

"We will do our best and leave the rest up to God," replies David. "Deal!!!!" Stephen smiles and says!!! The captain makes his announcements. The stewardess walks the aisle to make sure everyone is buckled up. As the plane taxis to the runway, it fires all engines on high and barrels down the runway. As the plane lifts off the ground, David sits and thinks of home and his family. Then his mind goes to his tryout with the Leafs. Then he thinks to himself many people on this plane have many dreams, but this was the beginning of the journey for his biggest one!!

Miracle From First Pit Pond

Chapter 11: Hello, Toronto!!!

"Ladies and gentlemen, this is your captain speaking. In about seven minutes we will be making our descent into Toronto. The skies are clear and sunny with headwinds out of the west. Current temperature in Toronto is -6C. Sit back, relax and we will have you on the ground shortly."
"David have you ever been to Toronto?" Asks Stephen.
"No, buddy, I haven't," replies David. "How about you?"
"Well two summers ago, my cousin Mathew and I left one Sunday after church, he drove a truck, we delivered lumber in Buffalo, New York, late Monday morning. Did two pickups of steel in Toronto Tuesday morning. Tarped it and went down the road, grabbed a shower and our supper and we delivered in Woodstock, New Brunswick on Wednesday morning around 10:30 am in the morning. Then we came home. It was a long drive but a fun trip. And that's the one and only time I have been to Toronto," replies Stephen, "besides, now." "But I do know it's a petty big city! Most teams with an NHL franchise are," replies David. "Well this is exciting isn't it?" David smiles and asks.
"For sure, pal," replies Stephen as the plane pulls up to the gate and the cabin door opens. David and Stephen walk up there connecting hanger as they enter the airport, they see a sign that says baggage claim to the right.
"That's us," replies Stephen.
"Yes, sir," David says. As Stephen and David grab their suitcases, off the carousel, they look and notice a man with a long black trench coat. He is smiling and holding a sign that says "Gallagher and Theriault". David approaches and says "hello sir, how are you?"

"Just fine," the man replies. "Is it David Gallagher and Stephen Theriault you are looking for?"
"Yes, young man. That's correct," he replies. David waves Stephen over, then he sticks out his hand to the man in the trench coat. "Nice to meet you sir, I'm David Gallagher."
The man smiles and shakes his hand. "I'm Gary, nice to meet you as well!" Stephen comes up and extends his hand, " hi, I'm Stephen, Stephen Theriault."
"Hi Stephen, I'm Gary, I will be your guy's chauffeur today!"
"Great," replies David.
"So you guys have your suitcases?" asks Gary.
"Yes, sir," Stephen replies.
"Ok, then," Gary smiles and says "let's roll!"
They go to the car and Gary opens up the trunk and puts in the boys suitcases. As David opens his door and sits behind the driver. Stephen walks around to the passenger side front of the car. He opens the door and replies as he sits down. "This is a nice car, what kind is it?" The driver smiles and replies "well thank you very much. It's a 1985 Chrysler, New Yorker."
"Cool, says Stephen as he fastens his seat belt.

Gary starts the car, looks out the drivers side mirror, before merging into the traffic. As he exits the airport and enters out onto the road, he hands the boys two envelopes. "Here you go guys!"
"What are these? Asks David. "It's your gentleman's itinerary. Times I pick you guys up directions to some nearby restaurants with Maple Leafs charge accounts by the way so when you go to eat sign and print your home and charge it to the Leafs!" Gary smiles and says. "And your motel room numbers."
"Wow, awesome, thanks," replies David. "Ya, thanks Gary," says Stephen. "You're welcome," replies Gary. "welcome to the big leagues guys!!" It's real nice of Mr. Nicols and the Leafs to do all this stuff for us," replies David.
"I have been doing chauffeur work for over seven years for the leafs and one thing I will say is whether you're a member of the team or a new prospect, the Leafs treat everyone one hundred and ten percent."

"Wow thats cool!" replies Stephen. As they talk and drive before long, they pull up to the Windsor Arms Hotel.
"Here ya go guys," says Gary. "Enjoy your stay and I'll be out front to get ya's at 8:00 am sharp, please don't be late."
"We won't, sir" says Stephen. Gary pulls the car in park and opens up the trunk. The boys grab their suitcases and say "Thanks for everything," to Gary. David says "it was great to meet you Gary!" "You as well guys," Gary smiles and says. As the boys begin to walk away, Gary yells out to them. "Guy's get lots of rest tonight!" "You have a big, big day tomorrow!!" "We will Gary, thanks for everything," replies David. "My pleasure," Gary smiles and says. As he gets back into the New Yorker and pulls away. The boys check into their rooms and unpack. "David can I ask you a question?" "Sure," replies David. "Does any of this seem real to you? Like it almost feels like a dream, doesn't it?" "I know buddy, it's pretty amazing," says David. "I hope you get signed after you are observed tomorrow." "One step at a time my friend, one step at a time," replies David. "Do you ever think you may get signed or offered to sign before I do?" David asks Stephen. "What, you're crazy!!" Stephen replies. David looks angry and quickly throws rolled up tube socks at Stephen's chest hard and fast. Stephen quickly knocks them away with his hand, before they ever hit his chest. David quickly runs towards Stephen, Stephen steps back quickly. David wasn't a giant in stature, but he was very very well able all he ever did was farm work, played hockey, shoveled snow and mowed lawns to make extra money, so he was more than able, especially if he was angry. David stops quickly about two and a half feet in front of Stephen and quickly raises his fsit and takes a fighting stance. Stephen backs up and doubles up his fist and takes a fighting stance to defend himself! David lowers his fist, smiles and says," I'm not mad pal, but I did what I did to prove a point. I threw tube socks at you hard and fast, before they even got to you, you knocked them away with your hand! I ran towards you, youstepped back quickly. I raise my fist, you took a fighting stance. That's the point I'm trying to make. You reflexes work extremely well and are extremely fast!! That's what a great goalie needs, and that's what you got!!! "Thanks!!" Stephen smiles and says. "The good Lord above blessed you with a cat like, reflexes

not everyone has that you know!" David smiles and says. "Thanks pal," replies Stephen. "Let me ask you a question. How do you see all these things that people miss?" ask Stephen to David. "Well I don't really know my friend. I just guess that I'm really, really, observant. Tomorrow you just remember to relax your right leg a little and no matter what anyone does or says do not feel intimidated!!"
"I won't," Stephen smiles and replies! "Hey David," says Stephen. "Ya buddy," David replies. "Thanks for being a great friend!" "My pleasure kid!!!"
"Hey, you're only six months older than me."
"Six months and four days," replies David. Both boys giggle. "See ya in the morning buddy, I'm heading for the shower."
"Later, tater," says David. As David turns the TV on, lies on his bed and watches a hockey game Habs, playing the Flyers. As he watches, he drifts off to sleep as he lays in his bed. The Flyers were up to three to one when he fell asleep. He awakes as the third period is down to five minutes and change. The Flyers are leading five to four as he awakes. He thinks to himself, as he watches the game. I have studied just about every player from both of these teams. I don't think there is much more I can learn by watching them. As the final three second remain, the Habs knock one in, but the goalie stops it. The Flyers win five to four. David shuts off the TV and gets down on his knees to pray. "Dear Lord, please give me a good peaceful rest. I pray for all my friends and family back home tonight. And I pray for everyone worldwide that is hurting tonight. Please comfort them and help them. Thank you so much for this opportunity, you and Mr. Nicols has given me to make a dream of mine come true. And Lord if it is your will, please let them sign me tomorrow. In Jesus' name Amen." He gets in his bed and closes his eyes and drifts off to sleep. At 6"30 am Stephen excitedly is beating on David's door. "David, open up the door." Yawning, "Morning pal, what time is it anyway?" "It's 6:30 am sharp," replies Stephen. "What do ya think about going for a twenty minute jog right now, loosen everything up before our big day then come back have a nice continental breakfast and get ready for our big day." Sounds great buddy," replies David. "I'll meet

you in the lobby in five minutes." "Great!!!" Stephen smiles and says! After they return from their lovely jog, they go into the dinning area and get their breakfast. The boys are so much alike. David grabs scrambled eggs, pork sausage, and a bowl of Special K. One glass of milk and one glass of orange juice. Stephen's was the exact same except he got apple jack's for his cereal. The boys woof their breakfast meal into them quickly as most teenagers do. "It's 7:25 am," says Stephen. "We better get up to our rooms and get ready." "That's right," says David. The boys go up to their rooms. Stephen washes up and changes into fresh clothes, while David jumps into the shower very quickly. As David finishes getting dressed and sprays a little cologne on, he looks at the clock 7:51 am. Good, he thinks to himself right on time. As David grabs his gym bag and goes out the door Stephen is waiting with his and gives a friendly wave. As they leave the Windsor arms, and walk out to the sidewalk, David checks his wrist watch 7:56 am. "No sign of Gary yet, huh?"asks Stephen. "No, not yet! David smiles and says, "but it's only four minutes till 8:00 am. As the boys stand on the sidewalk and look way down the street, they see a big black Chrysler New Yorker coming. And as it approaches, they hear what seems to be a friendly honk coming from it. "There's Gary," Stephen smiles and says. "Yep and rate on time it's 7:59 am," replies David. Gary pulls up to the curb, and gets out and opens the trunk. The boys put their gym bags in it. "Good morning, gentlemen!!" Gary smiles and says! "Good morning Gary, how are you doing today?" asks Stephen. "Listen i'm doing so well, I gotta sit on my hands to keep from clapping!" They all share a giggle!! "Ha, ha, ha, that's funny," replies Stephen. The boys get into the back of the New Yorker, and put their seat belts on. "Would you guys like a donut?" asks Gary. "Sure, that would be great!" replies David. As Gary hands the box back, David grabs his favorite, an apple fritter, Stephen grabs a double chocolate. "Hey, thanks a million Gary!" replies Stephen. Gary smiles and says, "you're welcome." As Gary pulls back into traffic and begins to drive down the road, he asks the boys, "so guys, how do you like your hotel?" "Awesome, just awesome!" says Stephen. "Ya it is great," says David. "Ya the Windsor Arms is great!" replies Gary. "My wife and I went there for a weekend to celebrate our fifteen year wedding anniversary." "Oh, nice, how long have you and your wife been married?" asks Stephen. "Nineteen years this may," replies Gary. "Well that's just great!" says Stephen. "Thanks," replies, Gary. "So David are you nervous about today?" asks Stephen. "No I'm just gonna do my best," replies David. "That's the spirit!" replied Stephen. "How did you sleep?" asks David. "Oh, just great," says Stephen. "How about you David?" "Oh, I slept really really well. My bed in my room is very, very comfortable.

Gary says "hey guys, just think in a day or two, ya's may be official Maple Leaf team members. I know it's very exciting," says Stephen. "Oh, for sure guys," replies Gary. "And if ya's are, you will both be on your way to training camp, the first week in July!" replies Gary. "The first week in July?" asks David. Gary chuckles. "No, no, no, don't worry it actually begins on August seventh. You know you gotta have a little summer vacation now." "Yea, I suppose," replies David. "Three more city blocks and we will be there guys," says Gary. "Man this is so exciting, and unbelievable!!" says David. "Ya tell me about it!" Stephen smiles and says. As they pull up in front of Maple Leaf gardens, outside waiting is Mr. Larry Nicols, smiling brightly. David looks at his watch at 8:47 am. Mr, Nciols opens the back passenger side door and says "good morning," The boys both reply "Good morning," in unison to him. Gary shuts the car off and opens up the trunk. Mr. Nicols looks at his watch. "Right on time Gary, we appreciate that!" He smiles and says. "No problem Mr. Nicols," replies Gary. Gary smiles, " how is your day so far, sir?" "Great, just great," says Larry.

"Good luck today guys!" Gary smiles and says. "Thanks Gary," says Stephen. "We appreciate it," says David. "Have a great day, everybody," Gary smiles and says as he gets in his car and drives away. "Come on in guys," Larry smiles and says "there's a couple people I want ya's to meet." As the boys walk into the gardens, they look around in awe and wonderment. "So guys, are you very excited for today?" asks Larry. "Oh, just around a forty four out of ten," says Stephen. Mr. Nicols and the boys chuckle. "Well we are very excited for today, as well!" says Larry. "What do you mean by we?" Asks David. "Me and the two gentlemen you're gonna meet here in a minute." As they walk and talk, they round a corner and walk past a large sign that says "Maple Leaf Gardens Action Guaranteed" As Stephen reads it, he says, "Hey David what do you make of that sign?" "I'm not one hundred percent sure pal, what do you think about it?" "Hard hitting, fast NHL action would be my guess," replies Stephen. "I'm not sure," replies David. "I have a different take on it." "Oh, what would that be?" asks Stephen. "Well the action of the pursuit, for the Stanley Cup," replies David. "Guys this is the room we are going into," Mr, Nicols says. "Interesting take on that sign," says Larry to David. "Thanks, Mr. Nicols," he replies as Larry opens the door, and Stephen and David are greeted by two friendly smiling faces. "My/ Gerry McNamara and Mr. Al Lafrate, of the Toronto Maple Leafs." "Nice to meet you guys," David smiles and says. "Yes it is," Stephen smiles and says. David extends out his hand and Larry says, "guys this is Mr. Gerry McNamara general manager of the Maple Leafs and Mr. Al Lafrate defense man with the Toronto Maple Leafs." "Nice to meet you Mr. McNamara, I'm David Gallagher" as he shakes his hand. Stephen sticks out his hand, "nice to meet you Mr. Lafrate. I'm a big fan," says Stephen. As David shakes Al's hand and Stephen shakes Gerry's hand, both Mr. McNamara and Mr. Lafrate tells the boys it's nice to meet them. "How have all your accommodation and everything been?" asks Mr. McNamara. "Just great, sir," replies David. "Yes we are really happy with them," replies Stephen. "Thank you very much," replies Stephen. "Yes, thanks," says David. "Guys I believe as Mr. Nicols told you the Leafs are out on the road today and Mr. Lafrate here is gonna try to score some goals on you Stephen." "Yes, why aren't you out on the road with the team?" asks David to Al. "I was checked pretty hard into the boards, bruised up my hip pretty badly. But I got released yesterday by the doctor to play again. But Mr. McNamara asked me to hang out here today and work with you guys." Al smiles and says. "Yes, he's gonna see if he can get a few goals past you Stephen," says Mr. McNamara. "Wow!" replies Stephen. "I'll do my best to stop them!" Everyone laughs. "That's the spirit," says Mr, Nicols. "Well guys let's get to the dressing room, suited up and out on that ice!!" "Sounds great," replies Daivd to Mr. Lafrate. Mr McNamara and Mr. Nicols sit exactly five rows up from the centerline on the west side of the building. "Ok," says Mr. McNamara, the first three shots do what you want, your choice." "Ok Mr.Namara," replies Al. He drops the puck on the centerline and skates up to the opposite blue line from where Stephen is. He skates down hard and fast and grabs the puck off the centerline. And barrels towards Stephen. Stephen flexes his right leg back and forth a little like David taught him. Al goes in hard and fast to the left side about twelve to thirteen feet out. Al smashes the puck with his stick hard, fast and high to the right hand corner of the net. And Stephen makes a beautiful glove save. "Great save," shouts out Al. "Way to go Stephen!!!" shouts out David from behind the bench. "Thank pal," shouts out Stephen. "Ready to go again?" asks Al. "Yes, sir," replies Stephen. Stephen throws the puck out of his glove to the right hand corner. Al grabs the puck and skates out hard to the centerline and turns very quickly. He skates hard, just into the edge of the blue line Stephen is watching Al's arm movements. Al lets a slapshot go, hard and fast. The puck is between the right goal post and Stephen's right leg. It was Stephen's quick reflexes that caused him to drop his pad down quickly. It bounces out fast and hard and quick as a cat. Al is right here ready to bang it in, but Stephen covers it over just in the nick of time with his glove. "Great save young man," hollers Mr. McNamara," from the seats on row five. Stephen takes his stick and taps it out to the left. Al skates up past the blue line, skates down fast and hard towards the net. He gets about a foot from the net, Al flips a wrist shot up and Stephen does his best to block it, but it just goes past his right shoulder. Stephen skates out and shakes hands with Mr. Lafrate. "Great goaltending today, Stephen." "Jeez thanks Mr. Lafrate." "Just call me Al," he smiles and says. "I love how you flex your leg back and forth a bit, for two reasons. Number one it's kinda distracting to me as a player. You're smart to do that," replies Al. "And number two, you're making it loose and flexible, moving it to warn it up so you can quickly move it! It's a great idea, where did you ever learn that?" asks Al. "From him." Stephen points to David." "Nice work out

Miracle From First Pit Pond

there buddy," as Al and Stephen skate up to where David is sitting. "I'm impressed with what you taught Stephen about moving his leg," replies Al. "Thanks a lot, Mr. Lafrate," says David. Al smiles, "just call me Al." They all giggle. Stephen is just grinning with positive energy. Up in row five, Larry asks Mr. McNamara a question. "Well sir, what do you think?" Mr. McNamara replies "two out of three, not bad. Especially for a kid off a pond in New Brunswick. So what are you thinking now, Larry?" Asks Mr. McNamara. "Well sir, I was thinking get David out on the ice, keep having Al trying to score goals, see how David does on the defense!" "Sounds great, Larry," replies Mr. McNamara. "David," called out Larry. "Yes Mr. Nicols," replies David. "Get out on the ice. Take three laps around quickly, warm up a little. We want you to stay between Stephen and the blue line. Do your best to stave off Al ok?" "Ok, sir," shouts out David. "Go David," Stephen shouts out as David jumps over the boards. "Ha, ha, ha," laughs McNamara, just like an NHLer already jumping over the boards." David takes three laps quickly around and stops about four feet in front of Al. "Wanna catch your breath?" asks Al. "Naaa, let's play some hockey," replies David. "Take it easy on me now," says David. "I'm just a rookie." "Young fella, what I hear from those guys up in the stand, you better take it easy on me." As he winks at David, Al takes the puck and skates to the opposite blue line, he comes barrelling down the right side, David skates backward and glances back at Stephen's net quickly. He tries to check Al but he misses as Al moves quickly as a cat and gets off a slapshot. Stephen blocks it with his chest and the puck bounces out in front of the net crease area. David grabs the puck quickly with Al hot on his trail. David fires it up past the centerline Al skates up, grabs it and heads down to the left of David. Al turns to the right quickly and goes to check David. David moves quickly and turns fast, checking Al, knocking him to the ice, and skates all the way past the centreline, fires a shot and it goes into the opposite empty opposing net. As the guys continue to scrimmage with Al, Mr McNamara leans over to Larry and says " Larry i've seen enough, how about getting Al and David to go against Stephen hard and fast. See what he can do with two guys." "Ok, sir," says Larry. Larry takes his whistle out of his pocket and blows it. Larry says "hey guy, clear out to the center line, we wanna see a lot of passing, a lot of movement. Hard and fast pour it onto Stephen with all you got. "Ok, sir," replies David. David fires the puck over to Al, he skates out past the center line. Him and David make the approach towards Srephen. Al passes to David, David is about twenty feet out from Stephen, David fakes a shot, hits the puck over to Al with his skate. Al fires one in, Stephen goes down and barely blocks it. It bounces out David flips a hard quick wrist shot into the air, Stephen raises his stick quickly and deflects it off. It bounces to the left side. David is right there and passes it over to Al. Al slaps one in hard. Stephen just got up and bounced off his right arm. David shoots around the back quickly, takes the puck and pokes it in past Stephen quickly. Larry blows his whistle, leans over to Mr. McNamara ``well sir, what do you think?" "I'd say it's exceptional playing by that young goaltender, that is what I think. Two out of three isn't bad but three out of four is ever better," replies Mr. McNamara. Larry grins and nods his head. He blows his whistle again. David skates hard and fast to the center line. He fires it down to Al who is about five feet from the approaching blue line. Al fires a slapshot that bounces off Stephen's left pad. David is right there, he slaps one in. Stephen blocks it again before the puck gets a chance to bounce, Stephen falls on top of it. Mr. Nicols blows his whistle again. "Guys all three of yas line up on the centerline, please," asks Larry. Al, Stephen, and David all line up on the center line. As Larry walks down to the ice, he says, "Al skate down to Stephen's net with me." "Sure, Mr. Nicols," replies Al. David and Stephen begin to talk amongst themselves. As they look down and see Mr. Nicols and Al taking by the net, David asks Stephen. :I wonder what they are talking about?" "I'm not sure," says Stephen, but I'm having a blast! How about you David? Isnt this arena beautiful?" asks Stephen. "It's great!!," replies David. "Can you imagine playing hockey here everyday?" "Keep playing the way you're playing, you just may!!" David smiles and says. "Thanks, buddy!" "No problem Stephen, my good man!" The boys share a chuckle. Mr. Nicols points up at Stephen and smiles. Al skates back up to the centerline, Mr. McNamara walks over to the penalty box, and returns walking to the centerline with a large box.

"Boys, how are ya feeling?" asks Mr. McNamara. "Great!" replies Stephen.``Just fine," David smiles and says. Mr. McNamara reaches into the box and throws a puck up the ice. Then he gently tosses another one by his feet then he throws a couple seven feet to the left then he kicks a couple down towards the blueline, then he checks one over his shoulder. "Boys take your gloves off and come over here," asks Mr. McNamara. The boys lay their gloves on the ice. Mr. McNamara says "guys, put two pucks a piece in each hand, go roughly three feet to the left and to the right and place a puck on the centerline roughly ever three feet." Mr. Nicols jumps over the left hand sideboards about seven feet from the edge of the goalies crease with something in his hand and stands grinning. "What's going on?" asks David to Mr. McNamara. "Well boys, Mr. Nicols is standing there with a radar gun, we are gonna have Al fire a slapshot from the centerline and see what is registering on the gun." Al takes his stance. "All ready sir," says Al to Mr. McNamara. "Ok, Al, fire away at will!" He lifts his stick at the top tip just by his kidneys and brings it down hard and fast! The puck soars down the ice and it goes in just to the left of the goal post on the left. "Well," Mr. Nicols asks Mr. McNamara, " what do you think?" "well it was really sailing," replies Mr. McNamara. "Had to be seventy six or seventy seven miles per hour." "You're not far off sir, eighty miles per house to be exact." " Very nicely done, Mr. McNamara," replies to Al. "Thank you sir!" replies Al. "ok David," says Mr. McNamara, "there should be roughly twelve pucks from the center to the left or right minus that one Al fired. There are eleven on each side sir," replies David. "No problem, we went a little wider than expected, but that's ok. Ok David pick a side from center. Hit them down left or right t doesn't matter,but don't stop till you run out of pucks on your side you pick, ok?" "Ok, Mr. McNamara," replies David. "Good luck David!" shouts Stephen. "Thanks pal!" David smiles and says. David takes a firing stance. "At your whistle Mr. Nicols." Larry blows the whistle and David hits one puck after another. He gets done and skates to the upper blue line and back to center. "Well Mr. Nicols, did he hit seventy five miles per house with one or two?" "No sir, no he did not," replies Larry. As Mr. McNamara unwraps a piece of double mint gum and puts it in his mouth as he begins to chew he says "well it had to be at least seventy miles per hour, it looked like they were really sailing." "No sir, it was not seventy miles per hour." "Well what was it then?" asks Mr. McNamara. Mr. Nicols looks up and smiles brightly with his notepad. "Puck one, sir was ninety miles per house. Puck two, ninety two miles per hour, puck three ninety three miles per hour, puck four and five ninety four miles per hour. Puck six and seven, ninety five miles per hour. Puck eight and nine, ninety six miles per hour, puck ten, ninety six miles per hour and puck eleven, ninety seven miles per hour." "Whoa!!!" replies Al. "Double whoa!!!" Mr. McNamara smiles and says. "Way to go David, Stephen smiles and says!" "Thanks buddy" David gives a wink and a nod. "Al what is your current weight?" asks Mr. McNamara. "198 lbs sir," "and you're six feet?" "No sir, 6'1"." "David I remember looking at your paperwork. You're 5'10" right and is it 156lbs your weight?" "No sir," replies David, "it was 155lbs, but I weighed myself in the locker room in my underwear before coming out here. "What is it now?" asks Mr. McNamara. "159 lbs." "Beefing up ay, young man?" asks Mr. McNamara. "I don't know, I think it's all in my arms. Those five gallon buckets of milk from our farm without the cream separated yet are mighty heavy!!" They all giggle and laugh. "Ha, ha, ha ,ha, keep carrying that milk," replies Mr. McNamara! "I haven't see this kind of strength and endurance since Doug Gillmore's rookie year!!" replies Mr. McNamara. "Stephen please get back in the net," says Mr. Nicols. "Ok, sir," replies Stephen. "David please skate down picking up a puck from anywhere, and as you approach Stephen, please show Mr. McNamara your swirling puck motion. Once you get past the blue line, try to score anywhere between there and the net." David smiles as he starts to skate past the blue line, he shouts to Mr. McNamara, "fire at will, sir?" Mr. McNamara giggles and says "yes David. Fire at will!!!" David skates back out past the center line and turns and goes back towards the blue line. Stephen is watching him like a hawk. Stephen gets between the blue line and left side swirling, swirling and let's go a wrist shot hard and fast. Stephen blocks it with his stick just barely. David looks back and sees how Stephen blocked it. He skates hard and dast going up to the upper right hand corner of the visitors end. He grabs a puck and skates back down toward Stephen. Swirling and swirling the puck. He gets almost to the blue line and he fires a slapshot on net, hard and fast. Stephen drops to his knees to block it, but he is just a split second too late. "Nice goal David!" says Al. "Thank you, sir." Mr. McNamara shouts down to David. "David how are you doing down there?" "Just fine, sir," replies David. "Ok Al and David, take every puck you see here on the ice. Fire them back and forth to each other, and fire at will on Stephen. Ok?" "Ok," says Al and David. David starts off swirling back and forth around the back of the net. He tries to poke one in around the side, but he fails. Stephen was tight against the post. Al slaps one in from the blue line. Stephen quickly drops to one knee and deflects it off his thighs. After three minutes straight of relentless pounding of pucks coming on him. Mr. Nicols blows his whistle. There are no pucks left from the blue line on up and you guys even hit the same one once three times. Very nice, very nice," replies Larry. "Mr. McNamara have you added up shots on goal yet?" "Yes, Mr. Nicols, forty eight shots on goal. Three goals scored by Al and two by David. Alright guys, nicely done," says Larry. "Hey Stephen!" calls out Mr. McNamara. "Yes, sir?" "That's over eighty seven percent goals saved of three minutes of steady shooting." "Is that good, sir?" Asks Stephen. "No, young man, that's great." Mr. McNamara smiles and replies. "Well Mr. Nicols, anything else today?" asks Mr. McNamara. "No, sir, I think we have covered it all." ". "Ok, guys, hit the showers," says Mr. McNamara. As the boys begin to skate off the ice, Mr. McNamara asks, "Hey boys are ya's looking forward to the big game Saturday night?" "Very excited!!!" replies Stephen. "Can't wait!!!" replies David. "Well we're glad you are and were happy and excited to have you and your friends here. Gary will be by in forty five minutes to pick you guys up out front in forty five minutes. And we will see ya's Saturday morning at 9:00am sharp. Gary will pick you up at your hotel at 8:15am sharp, Saturday morning." "Excuse me, sir," says David to Mr. McNamara." "Yes David," replies Mr. McNamara, what about tomorrow?" "What about it?" asks Mr. McNamara. "Well didn't you wanna see us tomorrow for more ice time?" "Oh, no,no,no young man, that won't be necessary. I think we've seen all we need to see until

Saturday. Don't you agree Mr. Nicols?" "Oh, I think so, sir," replies Mr. Nicols. "We have things to attend to guys." Mr. McNamara smiles and says. "Oh, by the way, guys. Tomorrow morning three blocks to the south of you, there is a street called Donaldson. on 2010 Donaldson, there was a little cafe called "Mike's Cafe". From 10:30 am till noon they have half priced Fridays, and heads up[guys they have one of the best warm ham and cheese sandwiches and blueberry muffins you will ever have in your life! Go down there tomorrow, get whatever you like, tell them to put it on Slow Pokes tab." "Who's slow poke, sir? Asks Stephen. "I am," Mr. McNamara smiles and replies. David recites a bible scripture "He that giveth unto the poor shall not lack: but he that hideth his eyes shall have many a curse." "That's right," Mr. McNamara smiles and says. "Proverbs 28:27." "That's right," David smiles and says. "Thank you for your kindness, sir." "Ya, thanks a lot," replies Stephen. "David, are you a Christian?" asks Mr. McNamara." "Yes, sir, for a little over four years now." "How about you?" asks David. "Yes, I am!" Mr. McNamara smiles and says. "How about you, Stephen?" Asks Mr. McNamara. "Yes, sir," replies Stephen. "But only two years for me. But Jesus and David are teaching me a lot!" "I'd say you are off to a great start boys!" Mr. Nicols and Mr. McNamara are smiling! "Where two or three are gathered in my name," says Mr. Nicols. "Matthew 18:20," replies Al. "Hey you guys are Christians too?" asks Stephen. "Ten years for me," replies Al. "Only one year for me," replies Mr. Nicols, but Mr. McNamara and Al are teaching me alot!" He smiles and says. "Well praise the Lord!" Stephen smiles and says. The whole group smiles and chuckles. "Better hurry boys, Gary will be here before too long." "Ok," David replies. "Thanks for everything," replies David. "Yes, thanks so much," says Stephen. "You're welcome guys," says Mr. McNamara. As the boys walk down the rubber padding to the dressing room, both David and Stephen stop at the same time and look back.

"Amazing, huh Stephen?"

"You got that right, buddy," says Stephen. They turn and walk towards the dressing room. "Stephen this is like a dream come true!"

"It's amazing!" Stephen smiles and says! David and Stephen take a shower, get dressed, and go out to the front of the arena. Gary is there waiting.

"Hi, guys!" Gary smiles and says.

"Hi, to you," replies David. "I hope you weren't waiting long," says Stephen.

"Na, I haven't even been here three minutes yet. It's nice to walk around a little anyways to stretch my legs," Gary smiles and says. The boys get in and Gary jumps behind the wheel and pulls away!

"Can I ask you a question?" asks Stephen.

"Sure," Gary smiles and says.

"How well do you know Mr. McNamara?" asks Stephen.

"Quite well," says Gary.

"Why, young man?"

"Well he told us about Mike's cafe," says Stephen.

"Ahhh," replies Gary. "A little piece of Heaven on earth. My wife and I go there at least once a month."

"Well, that's great," says Stephen. "He told us to go there tomorrow between 10:30 am and noontime, for half price Fridays."

"Yea, that's right!" Gary smiles and says.

"Well, he told us to order whatever we wanted and to put it on Slow Pokes tab."

"Ha, ha, ha, ha," Gary chuckles.

"He really, really likes you guys, I'd say!"

"Thanks," says Stephen. "But why do they call him Slow Poke?"

"Yea, I've been wondering the same thing," says David. "He doesn't seem to move too slow to me," says David.

"Well boys, it is actually quite a tale if you would like me to tell it," says Gary.

"We would love you too if you don't mind," says David.

"I'd be happy to," says Gary.

"Well let me start by asking you guys a question. Did you guys notice anything odd or different about Mr. McNamara's appearance?"

"Not, really," says Stephen. "He seemed like an average middle-aged to older guy to me. I mean his hairline is receding a bit, and I noticed a little gray on the sides of his head, but he must be at least forty-eight or forty-nine years old."

"Ha, ha, ha," chuckles Gary, "he would appreciate you saying that. Three weeks ago he celebrated his fifty fourth birthday."

"He looks very, very nice for his age," replied Stephen.

"Yes, he does," says David.

"That's very nice of you boys to say," says Gary.

"Excuse me guys," says David.

"Yes," replies Gary.

"I noticed something about him," says David.

"What would that be?" asks Gary.

"His hands are huge. When he shook by hand, my hand almost fell into his. I'm no heman or anything," says David, "but I got a pretty good size strong hand, and mine almost disappeared into his, when he shook my hand."

"Hey, I remember, mine did too," says Stephen.

"You got it guys," says Gary. "Well anyways, Mr. McNamara grew up about one hour and twenty minutes from Winnipeg in a place called Winkler, Manitoba. Not far from the USA border with the state of Minnesota. There are a lot of welding and machine shops in that area. To service the farming industry and to build farming machinery. Well, Mr. McNamara was the oldest of seven children. Well, his dad walked out on the whole family when Mr. McNamara was only eleven years old."

"That's horrible," says Stephen.

"I'm sorry to hear that," replies David.

"Yeah boys, that's why it's best to stay away from alcohol if at all possible. It's called the devil's brew for a reason."

"Amen to that," replies Stephen.

"Well with two kids at home under the age of three, the only job Mr. McNamara's mom was able to find was on Saturday night and Sunday night. Working as a waitress in a diner at 4 pm till close at midnight. Well, the family struggled along and at one point his mom almost couldn't get enough food to feed them all. This broke Mr. McNamara's heart, and so he decided to try and get a job to

Miracle From First Pit Pond

help his mom. Well Mr. McNamara applied everywhere and he couldn't find anything. Finally, he got a job on Saturday on a farm. He worked there for six months, and one day the owner of a tool and die shop came in to drop the owner of the farm off some parts. Mr. McNamara overheard the farmer and the owner of the tools and die shop talking. The owner of the tool and die shop said he was so busy that he had to add an afternoon shift to his factory. Well, Mr. McNamara asked him for a job. The owner asked him "aren't you in school?". "Yes sir" replied Mr. McNamara ``I'm third in my class." The tool and die owner said well I think I would keep going to school then. Mr. McNamara said "sir, my dad left us and I have six brothers and sisters. My mom works too but it's all she can do to feed and clothe us. I'm very very grateful to God for the job with Mr. Johnson here, but it's only on Saturdays. Sir, I have no intentions whatsoever of quitting school. I know and realize how important education is. But I promise you I can do the work of any man." "Mr. Johnson what would you say about all this?" asks the tool and die shop owner. "Well sir, I am one hundred and ten percent satisfied with him." "Well kid, I'll tell you what. What time could you be at my tool and die shop, Monday after school?" "Well sir, school is out at 3:15 pm sharp. You are located on Smith street correct?" "Yes, young man, 175 Smith Street." I can walk from my school to there in twenty minutes easily. So I can be there between 3:35 and 3:40 pm." Well listen, you be at my shop and ready to work for 4:00 pm sharp. I'll train you for a week. You can work on my second shift from 4:00 pm until midnight. If you can do the job, I'll pay you thirty-nine cents per hour." "Wow, that's over three dollars per day." "Yes sir," said the shop owner.
"Wow, that's not much money," replies Stephen.
"No it's not," says Gary, "but in that period of time, it was a very good rate, especially for a kid in school."
"So Mr. McNamara went into the shop and learned. How his hands got so big from 4:00 pm till midnight, summer, winter, spring, and fall?
"He cooled and pulled thirty-eight-pound thrasher pins out of moulds for eight hours. And sometimes in the summertime, he would work a few hours overtime, to make some extra money.

Now while he did all this, he still kept his Saturday job at Mr. Johnson's farm, went to church every Sunday, graduated high school with honors, and still found time to play his favorite sport."
"Let me guess," asks David, "hockey?"
"Yes, hockey, that's where his heart was!!"
"Wow, Mr. McNamara sure worked hard," replied Stephen.
"Yes, he did," replied Gary. "But the summer he graduated high school was the summer the horrible event happened."
"What happened?" asks David."
"Well he literally went to school, went to work, went to church and played hockey. In fact, Mr. McNamara is a really good baseball player too. But in the summer he would play an odd game of baseball here and there. But in the summer, he played road hockey a lot, and if there was nobody to play with him, he would fire on the net for two or three hours at a time in hopes of reaching his dream!"
"What was his dream?" asked Stephen.
"Why to play in the NHL of course," replied Gary.
"Well scouts for a university in DeLuth Minnesota had watched him play when he was in grade eleven. Well Mr. McNamara led his team to the Manitoba Championship that year, in goals scored. The second most assist in the whole province, provincial wide that year."
"Wait a second," replies David.
"Yes David," says Gary.
"You said Monday to Friday Mr. McNamara pulled the 4:00pm to midnight shift right?"
"That's correct," replies Gary.
"Ok, and on Saturday he worked for Mr. Johnson on the farm?"
"Yes, that's correct also."
"Ok, well how did he get to the games Monday to Saturday?"
"Ahh, good question," says Gary.
"Well Mr. McNamara had a God given talent for hockey, and the tool and die shop owner and Mr. Johnson both knew he was so good he might go pro, so on the evenings he had games or Saturdays when there was a game, the tool and die shop owner and Mr. Johnson would give him time off to go. Cause they knew if he

got into the NHL, they could help him even more than they were able to by employing him."
"Wow, Mr. Johnson and the tool and die shop owner were great people," replies David.
"The world's full of great people, David," says Gary. "Sometimes we just gotta look a little hard to find them!"
"Thanks Gary," replies David.
"You're welcome! Well anyways, the scouts from the university over at DeLuth Minnesota offered Mr. McNamara a four-year university scholarship under one stipulation."
"What was the stipulation?" asks Stephen.
"He had to play hockey for them and only them for all four years, but if he agreed to this they promised him an official viewing by NHL scouts."
"Wow, that's wonderful!!" Stephen smiles and says.
"I'll say," says David.
"Yes," replies Gary, "but two days after that offer, actually two days and two hours and thirty-four minutes exactly after that offer was when the tragedy struck."
"Oh, no, what happened?" asked David.
"Well once the offer was presented to Mr. McNamara, he said it sounded wonderful to him, and that he hadn't replied to any other universities yet because his boss at the tool and die shop said he could work there for a year, with the promise of a minimum of sixty-two hours a week because the tool and die shop was booming. And of course he would get time and a half pay after forty-four hours in a week. So Mr. McNamara thought this was a great way to save money for school for his secondary education. So as far as Mr. McNamara was concerned, he would accept the offer from the scouts, he just wanted to talk with his mom about it first. So at 12:30 pm the next day, they all agreed with Mr. McNamara and the scouts to have lunch at the diner where his mom worked. And they all agreed that would be fine. Well, Mr. McNamara and his mom talked. She said to follow his dreams, and he had her blessing to go to University. So after they had lunch, they had an agreement in place, and they shook hands on it. The school officials said they would draw up the papers and mail them to him for him to sign and mail back. Well, Mr. McNamara went

home and enjoyed the day with his mom and siblings. And he went to bed early. So he got up and went to school feeling great! He had a great day at school. He walked to his job and was on the tool and die floor at 3:55 pm like he always done. Well, the day shift guy told him he had four crates all cooled and ready to be pulled out. Well without the day shift guys knowing, someone had grabbed the cold tray of thrasher rods but assumed they were a pile of hot ones. So they took the cold ones off the top and put them in the cooling water pool, assuming they were all hot and stacked the other steel crate of actual hot ones on the top!"

"Oh, no," cries out Stephen.

"When Mr. McNamara grabbed the thrasher rod in each hand, they were extremely hot. Thank the good Lord Mr. McNamara had extra thick leather gloves on. He dropped the rods immediately, but it was too late. He ran down to the foreman's office, he burst through the door and said to get him to the emergency room at the hospital, and fast. Both hands had second and third degree burns on them. Mr. McNamara peeled the gloves off each of his hands as he ran to the foreman's office. Well not only did Mr. McNamaa have second and third degree burns on both hands, it even damaged a lot of tendons and ligaments in his hands. So even lifting a hockey stick was out of the question.

"So they didn't honor his scholarship?" asks David.

"No, that's the amazing part of the story!" replies Gary. "The amazing part, because this is where God steps in!!"

"God?" asks David.

"God!!!!" Gary smiles and says. "Well he knew he was facing two or three surgeries to get everything in his hands put back into place, but after four or five-weeks Mr. McNamaras hands began to heal very, very fast. But all the doctors told him, he would never ever be strong enough in his hands to properly grip a hockey stick again. So when Mr. McNamara contacted the school officials and told them what happened, they felt horrible. So they told him over the phone that his scholarship agreement now was no good because he couldn't uphold his end of the bargain. But God was already involved and already in play. So you know how?" asks Gary to the boys.

"Well his hands were healing very fast," replied Stephen.
"Yes," replies Gary. "And that's definitely one way, but that's not the way I'm referring to. How else do you think God may have helped him?"
"I'm not sure," replied Stephen."
"Me either," says David.
"Well as I told you the school officials felt horrible for him, so they had a meeting and decided to redraft his scholarship."
"Wow!! Isn't that wonderful," says Stephen.
"I'll say!" replied David, "that's great!"
"Oh, Gary," says David.
"Yes," answers Gary.
"I'm loving this story."
"That goes double for me," says Stephen.
Gary smiles, "that's great guys! Well let me ask ya a question guy's," says Gary. "What do you think they redrafted his scholarship to?"
"I'm not sure," says David.
"Scouting?" asks Stephen.
"No," replies Gary, "but you're not far off."
"Well a four year all exclusive scholarship was written up and the only stipulation was that Mr. McNamara had to be head coach for the university of Minnesota at DeLuth for four years during his studies. Well, there were over seven schools in that division and over twenty-three in the whole midwest division. In four years, Mr. McNamara took them from a sixth-place finish in all the schools to number two in-state division championship."
"Wow, amazing," says David.
"Wait, there's more!" Gary smiles and says. "He never, ever needed skin grafts on his hands and the doctors also said his ligaments and tendons healed so good for such a horrible injury.
"That's amazing!!" replies Stephen.
"Amen!" David smiles and says.
"Well, when he shook our hands they seemed totally normal, except for the fact that they were so huge. I didn't see any scarring or anything," says David.

"That's the second miracle," replied Gary. "God divinely healed his hand, the ligaments, the tendons and the appearance of them. You can't even tell they were burnt so badly."
"That's really amazing," says Stephen.
"God is so good!!!"
"He sure is!" says Gary.
"Amen to that!" David smiles and says.
"Well the story isn't over yet guys," says Gary. "In his physical therapy, his doctor felt it would be good to get a pair of the hand squeeze grips and do seven reps each hour for thirteen hours every day. So Mr. McNamara started with seven reps every hour, but before too long, he was up to twenty-five rep per hand. And he still has them at his desk and uses them every day. But guess what?"
"What?" asks David.
"He does eighty-nine in a row with his right hand and eighty-five with his left hand. He's getting older and says he just doesn't have the strength he used to."
"He's doing great," says David.
"My hands are strong. I play hockey all the time and have been doing farm chores for over nine years and I can only do forty-one in a row, with my right hand and thirty-nine in my left.
"Ha, ha, ha, you got a way to go to catch him," says Stephen to David.
"I'll say," David chuckles and says.
"Well the other great part of the story is the university did bring the NHL to Mr. McNamara, but not scouts, franchise owners."
"What do you mean?" asks David.
"Well Mr. McNamara completed university with a business degree and the first job he got was head coach for the Chicago Black Hawks. He was five years with Chicago. And then four years with the Philadelphia Flyers. And then two years as head coach for the New York Rangers. Then after the New York Rangers, he got hired by Toronto Maple Leafs as their head coach and remained in that position until he became general manager of the team three years ago."
"Well how did he do coaching?" asks Stephen.
"Just great," replies Gary.

Miracle From First Pit Pond

"One Stanley Cup for Chicago, one for Philadelphia and year division leader for New York."

"Wow, awesome!" replies Stephen.

"But none for the Leafs?" asks David.

"Yes, that's correct, but let's hope you guys can help with that!!" Gary smiles and says.

"Gary, can I ask you a question?"

"Sure," replies Gary to Stephen.

"Do you really think we got a shot of the Leafs wanting us?"

"Of course I do!" Gary says with a smile. "Otherwise Mr. McNamara and Mr. Nicols wouldn't go through all the time and expense of having you here."

"Well, thanks," replies David.

"You're welcome," replies Gary.

"And thanks for the awesome story about Mr. McNamara," says Stephen.

"But Gary, your story was excellent," says Stephen, "but it still doesn't tell us why or how he got the name Slow poke."

"Ya, that's right," replies David.

"My apologies guys, I'm sorry." says Gary. "They nicknamed him Slowpoke because when he played he was fast as lightning.

"And you timed it great too," replied Stephen. "Here is our hotel just up ahead."

"Well guys, have a great afternoon and evening," says Gary. "If you need me tomorrow just call the office."

"No, I think we will do a little sightseeing tomorrow by foot," says David.

"Ya, and go to Mike's cafe too?" says Stephen.

"Most definitely buddy," replies David.

"Well you guys enjoy yourself, be careful and just call me if you change your mind. And remember I'll be here at 8:00 am sharp Saturday morning to have you over for practice with the team for 9:00 am."

"That's what they want us to do?" asks Stephen.

"Yes, Mr. Nicols told me when I dropped you guys off at the Gardens this morning."

"Wait," David says as he exits the New Yorker. "When you dropped us off before Mr. Namara or Mr. Nicols watched us play?"
"That's right," replies Gary. "Have a good one," Gary smiles and says."
"You, too," says Stephen.
David stretches out his hand to Gary.
"Gary, thank you for everything and God bless you."
"God bless you too," says Gary. He pulls the New Yorker in drive and slowly pulls away.
Stephen says to David, "What a great morning!"
"You can say that again pal," replies David.
"I'll go brush my teeth, then we will go for a walk and get a treat at the store."
"Ok, buddy," replies David.
"I'm gonna call my mom while you are brushing your teeth, Stephen." David goes into his room and picks up the phone. "Yes, operator a collect call from David, please."
"Hi mom, how are you?" says David.
"Great, sweetheart, nice to hear from you. How is everything going?"
"Great mom! We had our first ice time today. They said to us they have seen all they need to see for now and they want us to be at practice with them Saturday morning. No mom, tomorrow we are gonna go sightseeing," replies David. Hey mom, you should have seen Stephen today, he was amazing in net! No mom, nobody's gotten an offer yet. Ok Mom, I love you too!! Tell everyone at home I say hi and I love them!! I will call you tomorrow night. Bye mom, I love you very, very, much!!"
Stephen comes out into the hall smiling. "How is everything at home buddy?"
"Fantastic!" replies David.

The boys have a great afternoon and a great day of sightseeing on Friday. And a lovely sandwich compliments of Mr. McNamara at Mike's cafe. Saturday, they scrimmage with the whole team at practice on Saturday morning. Next thing you know it is 11:20 am

and practice is over. When they arrive back to the Windsor Arms Hotel at 1:15 pm and to their surprise LeRoy Gardner is waiting for them in the lobby in the big easy chair, drinking a can of Pepsi. "Well, hello boys!" LeRoy says with a big smile. "I thought I may not see you until tonight at Maple Leaf Gardens."
"Hi," says Darrell Cairns as he rounded the corner.
"Hi!!" David smiles and says.
"Anyways," LeRoy says, "we got here at 10:45 am and all checked in by 11:00 am."
"That's awesome!!" Stephen smiles and replies. "Yes and it was all paid for by Mr. McNamara," replied LeRoy. I believe he is the Maple Leafs general manager."
"Wow, how nice of him," replies David.
"I'll say," says Stephen. Darrell and LeRoy are shaking their heads in agreement. Around the corner, comes another familiar face.
"Look, it's Peter Eales," says David.
"Hi, Peter Eales," says David.
"Hi guys," Peter Eales smiles and says. "This is a nice place, huh?"
"Not too shabby," Stephen smiles and says. Darrell Cairns giggles "not too shabby, ha, ha, ha." The boys all break out giggling at Darrell.
"So guys any offers yet?" asks Darrell.
"No, not yet," says Stephen.
"I wish they would tell us something, even an indication of an offer," replies David. LeRoy puts his arm around David. "Patience is a virtue, my friend," says LeRoy. Peteral Eales smiles and says, "look who has a change of heart."
"Hey, we may be country bumpkins, but we are the best country bumpkins we can be!" LeRoy smiles and says.
"Amen, to that!" David smiles and says.
"Sometimes with frost on your pumpkin," says Stephen.
"Ya, but never in July and August," replies Darrell. The boys all share a laugh. "Well Let's grab some lunch then go to our rooms and get ready for the big game tonight!" LeRoy smiles and says. The boys all have a nice lunch together at a little diner not far from the hotel. Then go back to their rooms and get ready for a big, great night!! At 5:30 that evening, the boys are all outside the Windsor Arms Hotel.

"Hey, there's Gary now," shouts out Stephen. David runs to Gary's drivers door hard and fast. As the black New Yorker stops in the concierge area. David opens up Gary's driver's door with one hand and waves over all his friends with the other hand. The guys all run over quickly.
"Guys," says David, meet one of the best darned chauffeurs in Toronto!!!! Gary, meet the guys!" David smiles and says.
"Hi guys, pleasure to meet you all!" Gary smiles and says.
"Hi Gary, hi Gary they all say."
"Ok, there are seven of you guys, and I can only take four of yas so which three are gonna ride in the trunk?"
"What!!!" shouts out LeRoy Gardner.
"Ha, ha, ha, ha,ha!!! Gotcha!!" Gary smiles and says! All the boys chuckle at LeRoy.
"Hey Gary, are you gonna take four over, then come back to get the last three?" asks Stephen.
"It is Saturday night though and game night in Toronto!!! Would you have time to do it by game starting at 7:00 pm?" asks Stephen. All of a sudden a pretty middle aged blond lady pulls up in a red Ford Escort. She puts the car in park. Walks up to Gary and says, "hi, sweetheart!!" to Gary.
"Hi, sweetie," Gary smiles and says.
"Guys, Mrs. Gary. Mrs. Gary, the guys. She is also known as Tamara."
"Hi guys!" Tamara smiles and says. "Hi Tamara," they smile and say.
"Who's ready to go watch the leafs kick some butt?" asks Tamara.
"Ya!" the boys all cheer.
"Well four get in with hubby and three come with me. David, Peter, and LeRoy, jump in with Tamara, and the rest of the boys jump in with Gary."
As they arrive at Maple Leaf Gardens, Mr. McNamara is just inside the main entrance door with Mr. Nicols. As the boys walk in the door. Larry says with a loud voice and a big smile, "Good evening everyone and welcome to Maple Leaf Gardens!!!"
"Man, this is so exciting!!!" replies Brandon Copp.
"How was the flight up, guys?" Asks Mr. McNamara.

"Just great," replies LeRoy Gardner. LeRoy says to Peter Eales, "do you have it?"
"Yes," says Peter, as Brandon Copp, pulls one out of each of his pockets in his coat. LeRoy says, "Mr. Nicols and Mr. McNamara, we wanted to do something to say thank you for all your kindness to us. So go ahead Brandon," says LeRoy.
Brandon says, "Mr. McNamara, Mr. Nicols on behalf of all of us for all your kindness to us, we wanna present you with a bottle of homemade syrup, a piece, made from the maples of St. Croix, New Brunswick."
"Yes, sir we tapped the trees and boiled it down last year," replies Darrell Cairns.
"Aww boys, this is very, very kind of you Mr. McNamara," smiles and says, "Thank you."
"You're welcome," replies Marty Gardner.
"Yes, guys every Sunday before church is always pancake Sunday at our house," says Mr. Nicols. This will be just lovely on them! Thanks." The boys all smile and say, "you're welcome." The boys go in and take their seats. And just after the American and Canadian National Anthems, LeRoy shouts out and points to the big screen scoreboard in the center ceiling of the Gardens. "Guys, guys, look on the screen!!" The boys all look up at the board and read it as it says, "Maple Leaf Gardens would like to give a warm welcome to the First Pit Pond Miracles of St. Croix, New Brunswick." All of a sudden the announcer shouts out, "Ladies and gentlemen, boys and girls, please put your hands together and make some noise and give a big Maple Leaf Gardens welcome to Peter Eales, Stephen Theriault, Darrell Cairns, Brandon Copp, LeRoy Gardner, Marty Gardner, and David Gallagher all the way from St, Croix, New Brunswick attending their first NHL game tonight! Let's hear it for the First Pit Pond Miracles!!!"
All of a sudden, the building erupts in cheering and clapping. The boys are all smiling from ear to ear as wide as the Grand Canyon! What a great experience for young boys from rural New Brunswick. Mr. McNamara leaned over and said to Mr. Nicols, "I couldn't agree more sir," Larry smiled and said.
"Thanks so much for everything you did for them Mr. McNamara," Larry says with a smile. Mr. McNamara smiles wide

and says, "Larry the pleasure was all mine!!!" After the applauding and cheering dies down, the announcer says, "your officials for tonight are Henry Johnson, David Stiles, Troy Wood and Fred Jones." The whistle blows, the puck drops, and it's on. The boys had the time of their lives as they watched the game intently. The Toronto Maple Leafs hailed victorious over the St. Louis Blues four to three in overtime.

The boys get dropped off at their hotel and say goodnight to Gary and Tamara. They go inside the lobby, sit down together and talk about how awesome the game was. They're all sitting there and LeRoy says, "hey guys, let's all go up to my room and talk some more." "Sure," the boys say. As they all walk into LeRoy's room, Peter Eales asks David and Stephen. "No word from anyone tonight guys about anything?"
"No, not a word from anyone," replied David. "Maybe where it was game night they were extremely busy," replied Brandon Copp. "I don't know. I've thought about that," says David to Brandon. "Well what do you think?" asks Darrell Cairns to Stephen. "I'm not really sure," says Stephen. "But I'm like David. Even an indication one way or the other would be great!"
All of a sudden the conversation is interrupted by a phone call. LeRoy's room phone rings. The boys all become quiet. The phone rings again for a second time. LeRoy answers the phone. "Hello?" says LeRoy. "Yes," says LeRoy. "Yes, he is," says LeRoy. "Yes, just one moment, I'll get him for you. The boys all sit quietly. LeRoy says, Stephen, the phone is for you."
"Hello," says Stephen in his friendly voice. "Yes, this is Stephen Theriault. What's that?" says Stephen. Oh Mr. Nicols." The boys all listen very intently. "Yes we all loved the game, it was very nice of you and Mr. McNamara to bring us all the way here. Yes we all had a lot of fun sir. It was a blast! Tell David and the rest of the gang what? Ok, sir. Yes I will. Ok, Ok, thank you Mr. Nicols. God bless you too! Ok, goodnight now."
"Well what did he say?" asks Darrell Cairns as Stephen is handing up the phone. "Did he say it when they're drawing up the contracts?" asks Brandon.

Stephen turns and looks at all his friends. "Well?" says LeRoy. "He didn't say anything about a contract," says Stephen.
"Well what did he say?" asks Marty Gardner.
"He asked me if we all enjoyed the game. I said yes. He then said thanks to us all coming up and thanks for the maple syrup."
"Ok, then what?" asks LeRoy.
"He said checkout time is 12:00 pm sharp and Gary and another car and driver will be here at 12:20 pm to take us to the airport to catch our 3:45 pm flight."
"What? That's it?" asks Darrell Cairns.
"Yes, that's it," said Stephen.
"What the heck happened?" asks LeRoy. "I heard you guys did great."
"Where did you hear that from?" asks Peter.
"There were a couple guys checking out and told the front desk clerk they were friends with Al LaFrate and heard from him that there were a couple of young Maritime prospects here with great potential!"
"Really?" asks Brandon.
"Yes, really," says LeRoy. "I was sitting in the lobby and I heard them."
"Maybe, we just aint that good," replies Stephen.
"Aww, don't say that," replies Peter Eales to Stephen. Darrell Cairns looks over at David who is looking out the window, "David, what do you think?" David seems to be staring off aimlessly.
"Huh? What?" says David, to Darrell Cairns. "Are you ok?" asks Darrell. "I asked you what you think of all this?" David gets up out of his chair and says, "I think two things. Number one," as he pulls a five dollar bill out of his pocket, "across the way there is a store called Young's convenience, you go over there and get us a big bottle of Pepsi will you Darrell?"
"Sure, no problem," replies Darrell. "LeRoy we have two clean cups here in your room right?"
"Right," says LeRoy.
"Ok, grab the ice bucket will ya, and fill it down on the first floor and bring back five more styrofoam cups will ya?"

"No problem," says LeRoy. LeRoy leaves the room with the ice bucket.
"What's the second thing you know or think?" Asks Darrell.
"I know there is a movie on channel eight at midnight so get us some Pepsi and we will all watch it."
"Is that the second thing?" asks Brandon Copp.
David smiles brightly. He gets up and puts his arm around Brandon. "No Brandon, I just thought the movie and Pepsi thing would be nice. The second thing I think, I can't wait until 3:45 pm on Monday."
"What's going on at 3:45 pm on Monday?" Asks Stephen.
"I'll be at First Pit Pond to do what I love!! Playing Hockey!!"
"Who is gonna join me there?" David smiles and asks. Stephen walks over and smiles. "I'll be there too," replies Peter Eales. All the boys say they will be there.
"I'm sure LeRoy will be too, but he is currently on another assignment." The boys all laugh very loud and hard. Just at that moment, LeRoy comes back with an ice bucket full and five styrofoam cups.
"What? What did I miss?" asks LeRoy. The boys all giggle and laugh harder looking at LeRoy. David walks over to LeRoy and smiles and puts his arm around LeRoy and says, "Yes LeRoy, what you missed was me and the Miracles are gonna be at First Pit Pond at 3:45 pm Monday after school to play some good ol' Canadian pond hockey. Are you in?" asks David.
LeRoy smiles and replies, "Yaa, buddy!!!" All the boys giggle.
"What are ya's all laughing at me for?" Says LeRoy. Brandon Copp looks up and smiles, "Oh LeRoy, you're a comical soul that's for sure!" Darrell smiles and says, "I better go get the Pepsi, the movie is starting in a few minutes." Darrell leaves the room, and returns in a few minutes with a big bottle of Pepsi and some change for David. And after a night of cold Pepsi, laughs, and watching a great movie. The clock strikes 2:30 am. The boys all retire to their rooms. After a morning of a great continental breakfast and some more laughs amongst themselves, they pick up and check out.
"You know what?" says Peter Eales to Stephen and David.

"What's that? Asks David. "I'm sorry that Mr. Nicols and Mr. McNamara didn't tell you guys what was going on," he replies, "but man it was a great trip! Wasn't it?"
"It was," Stephen smiles and says! David puts one arm around Peter and one around Stephen and says, "guys this is a great memory, we will have our whole lives. I got a feeling with God's grace we will be pulling our grandkids up on our laps and telling them about this one day!!"
"Amen to that!!" Stephen smiles and says.
David is standing there with tears rolling down his face. LeRoy notices this and runs right over. "David, what's wrong?" LeRoy asks. "Maybe the Habs will give you a tryout next year. Don't be sad."
David giggles, "no Leroy, you don't understand," replies David. "I saw my favorite team play in our nation's biggest city. I learned a great, true story of love and perseverance and the man who went through all of it bought Stephen and I one of the best sandwiches I ever had in my life. And my best friends in the whole wide world are with me at this wonderful beautiful hotel. I'm not sad, LeRoy. I'm so blessed. And so lucky! And so fortunate to have what I have!! I love ya, buddy!!" David smiles and shouts with a loud voice, "and I love ya's too Miracles!!!
"We love you too, David!!" replies Brandon Copp.
"Hey, there's Gary," replies Darrell Cairns.
"And there's Mrs. Gary behind him again," says Marty Gardner.
"Hi guys," says Gary with a smile.
"Hello," the boys all smile and say.
"Sorry I'm a few minutes late," says Gary.
"Me and Tamara just got out of church."
"Oh, it's okay," says Peter.
"How was service?" asks David.
"It was just wonderful!!!" Gary smiles and says.
"We will be at our church next Sunday, good Lord willing," says David. Gary stops as he's loading the boy's luggage into the trunk. He looks up and smiles at David. "That's really great, David. My four best bits of advice, I can give you is don't drink, don't smoke, and don't do drugs. And no matter what life throws at you, always love and serve God and go to church."

"I will sir!!" David smiles and replies. "Ok, guys four in with me and three in with Tamara again," says Gary. "ok," says the boys. "Brandon, Stephen, and Darrell get in with Tamara. The rest get in with Gary."

"Hi, Mrs. Gary," says Stephen.

"Hi guys, how are ya's?" asks Tamara. "Just great!" says Tamara. "Well guys it was a pleasure getting to know you all," says Gary to his guys. "It was a pleasure getting to know you too, Gary!" says David.

"Gary, can I ask you a question?" says LeRoy.

"Sure," says Gary. "Well the Leafs general manager and the Leafs head scout bring Stephen and David all the way up here from New Brunswick give them a tryout, but then no word back after the try out. No indication of what they did wrong. No indication of what they did right. No meeting, no nothing, what's up with that?"

"Well," replies Gary, "Mr. McNamara and Mr. Nicols are extremely busy men. So my guess would be in a month or two they will get the secretary to write them a letter, thanking them for trying out."

"What? No interaction afterwards?" asks LeRoy. "That's crazy!" Replies LeRoy.

"Well kids, that's the hockey business and time is money."

"Well I'll be!" says LeRoy.

"Hey guys, don't let it get ya down," says Gary.

"Oh, we won't sir," says LeRoy, but it just seems strange to me." Gary and Mrs. Gary pulled up to the drop off area. The guys say thanks and their goodbyes to Gary and Mrs. Gary. Just as they grab their luggage and start to walk into the airport, a lady wearing an Air Canada uniform comes over to the boys and says, "excuse me, excuse me, is there a LeRoy Gardner here?"

"I'm LeRoy," LeRoy smiles and says.

"Ok," she says. "Is there a Stephen Theriault here?"

"I'm Stephen," Stephen smiles and says.

"Ok," she says. "And you are all part of a hockey team in New Brunswick? Umm....First Pit Pond Miracles?"

"Is there a problem, miss?" asks Peter Eales.

Miracle From First Pit Pond

"Yes I'm afraid there is," she replies. "Do you guys know Mr. Larry Nicols and Mr. Gerry McNamara?" she asks.
"Yes we do," says David.
"Well they cancelled your return tickets."
"What?" shouts out LeRoy Gardner.
Brandon Copp opens his wallet. Guys, I got seventy five, maybe that will get a couple of greyhound bus tickets to at least get a couple of us home, if we ask nicely."
"What about the rest of us?" asks Darrell Cairns. "If only two of us get home, I hope my mom and dad have the extra money to buy a plane ticket to get me home!!"
"I'm calling my mother collect right now," says Marty Gardner.
"Guys, guys, this has got to be some kind of mistake or misunderstanding," replies David.
"Oh, it's no mistake," says the Air Canada lady."
"Guys, listen," says Gary. "Let me and Mrs. Gary park the cars and we will go in with you and straighten this mess all out."
"Thanks, Gary!" says David.
"Yes, thanks, so much Gary," all the boys say.
"This is one of the many reasons why I love you, sweetheart!" says Mrs. Gary to Gary. "You always help people."
"Thanks, hun," replies Gary. Gary and Tamara find a couple parking spots and walk back over to the boys all in a span of about three minutes. As the boys, Gary, and Mrs. Gary, all go into the building, Gary says, "Ok guys, let me do all the talking, ok?"
"Sure," replies Stephen. They walk over to the lady who broke the news to them. "Miss there has to be some kind of mistake," says Gary.
"No, there is no mistake," she replies.
"But how on earth will these kids get home?"
"All of a sudden, the phone rings."
"Excuse me," says the lady.
"Hello, this is Julie with Air Canada," she says. "Hello, what's that?" asks Julie to the person she's talking to on the phone. "Well they will be glad to hear that," she smiles and says. "Ok, thanks."
"Well, what's going on?" Gary says to her. At this time, Tamara walks over, "well what's going on, dear?" she says to Gary.
"I'm not sure yet Tamara," replies Gary.

"Listen," says Julie. "I am sorry for the inconvenience, but there's a lady two rooms down on the left. Her name is Amber."
"Ok, thanks so much," replies Gary.
"She will go and help you. Just go down and see her."
"Ok, everybody, let's go," says Gary.
They all walk down the corridor and into the room. They are greeted by a friendly girl with a friendly smile. "Hi everyone, thanks for coming. I am Amber. I am with Air Canada. There are two men that are now gonna join us to tell you why your return ticket has been revoked. Ok?" Amber opens a door to the side, sticks her head in and says, "ok guys, they are all here and they're all ready." Out through the door comes Mr. McNamara and Mr. Nicols.
"Hi guys," says Mr. McNamara, just wanna say thanks again for that lovely New Brunswick maple syrup. It was delicious on my waffles this morning."
"Forget the waffles, what are you trying to do to us?" asks LeRoy Gardner.
"Don't be rude," Stephen replies to LeRoy.
All of a sudden Mr. McNamara, Mr. Nicols, Gary, Tamara and Amber all burst out laughing uncontrollably. Julie walks in and smiles. Julie smiles and says," here are your tickets to Fredericton, New Brunswick." As she gives them to Mr. Nicols, Mr. Nicols says, "thanks Julie."
"Julie you were in on this too?" asks LeRoy.
"Yes, I was dear, I'm sorry guys, have a great trip home." The boys breathe a sigh of relief and they all giggle. Darrell Cairns is laughing hard.
"You got us!!"
"You got us all good!!! You had us a little nervous there for a while Mr. McNamara," says David.
"Guys, I'm so sorry," says, Mr. McNamara "but we haven't won a Stanley Cup since 1967. We gotta do something to keep our spirits high and lifted around here, huh guys?" Mr. McNamara says to everyone on the job. Mr. Nicols walks up to David and Stephen and says, "this is a double sided meeting. We purposely didn't

meet with you after the practice on Saturday morning." The Air Canada employee exits the room.

"Thanks, Amber, you were awesome as usual!" replies Mr. McNamara.

"You're welcome, sir."

"Guys, have a great flight home," she smiles and says as she leaves.

"Continue on Mr. Nicols," says Mr. McNamara.

"Sure, sir," replies Larry.

"Well like I said, we knew we were gonna prank you guys, and also Mr. McNamara and I knew fifteen minutes into watching you both play the first day what we were going to do." Stephen's eyes got big, very big and bright!!

"Does this mean what I think it means?" asks Stephen.

"Well Stephen, we feel David is right. We do need better defense and goaltending in our organization. Maybe this is why we haven't won a cup since 1967."

Mr. McNamara and Mr. Nicols approach David and Stephen. Mr. McNamara says, "boys, Mr. Nicols and I was wondering if you would like to help us win a Stanley Cup and join the Toronto Maple Leafs?"

"Oh, my goodness," David says. He clutched his chest and stumbled backwards, bumping against a table. LeRoy runs over quickly. "David, are you okay?"

Mr. Nicols walks over as Darrell Cairns hands him a chair. He sets the chair under David and grabs him on his shoulder. "Here David, sit down." David sits down, looks up at Mr. Nicols, and smiles brightly. "I'm great, sir!!" replies David. "I just gotta catch my breath!" He says. Stephen is just standing there smiling brightly. All of a sudden, David stands on his feet. He walks over to Mr. McNamara, says "Trust in the Lord with all thine heart, and lean not unto thine own understanding. In all thy ways acknowledge him, and he shall direct thy path"

"Proverbs 3: 5-6," says Mr. McNamara.

"Yes, sir," David smiles and says. Larry walks up to Mr. McNamara and smiles. David extends his hand to Mr. McNamara, shakes it and smiles and says, "I'd be honoured to become a Maple

Leaf,". Stephen walks over and extends his hand to Mr. Nicols. "That goes double for me, sir."

"That's great guys," says Mr. Nicols. After Stephen shakes Mr. Nicols hand, he shakes hands with Mr. McNamara. Stephen extends his hand to Mr. Nicols.

"Thank you sir," David smiles and says, "thank you for all you've done for us.

"My pleasure," says Larry.

"God bless you, young man!" He gives David a big hug. "Always take care of that wonderful sister of yours."

He says, "I will, sir!!"

All of a sudden, Darrell, Brandon, Marty, LeRoy and Peter all erupt in massive cheering, excitement and joy! They all swarm David and Stephen.

"Whoa," says Mr. McNamara as he and Mr. Nichols barely escape the swarm. The boys all hug, embrace and cheer. LeRoy grabs David around his waist and picks him up. David hugs him. "You win that cup," says LeRoy, "I'll be hosting the barbeque sponsored in St.Croix, New Brunswick," replies LeRoy.

"I'm holding ya to that buddy," says David.

Mr. McNamara," LeRoy shouts.

Yes, LeRoy?" Mr. McNamara replies.

"Do you like lobster? Good maritime lobster?"

"Well yes I do," replies Mr. McNamara.

"Well when David brings that cup home to St. Croix, New Brunswick, come on down because I'm the guy throwing the Gallagher Stanley Cup homecoming!!! An all out barbeque with fresh lobster and seafood as well!!"

"Ok, you have a deal!!" says Mr. McNamara. As the guys get done cheering and embracing, Peter Eales says, "hey guys, we got a plane to catch and a practice at 3:45 pm Monday," he replies.

"At First Pit Pond!" David smiles and says.

"That a boy, David!" Mr. Nicols smiles and says. Gary walks over to the center of the room and says, "guys let's have a word of prayer before you hit the friendly skies."

"Sounds great," says Mr. McNamara.

Everyone comes full circle and joins hands. Gary says, " Mr. Nicols, will you lead us in prayer please?"
"Sure," replies Larry. "Lord bless each one of the boys here today. Thank you for allowing us to get to know them. And please keep your hands over each one of their lives. Give them a safe trip home. We ask all this in Jesus' name. Amen."
"Amen!" The boys all say in unison. Mr. Nicols, Gary, Tamara and Mr. McNamara all go over by the side door and shake hands with them all as they depart and head for their gate. Brandon Copp is the second from last guy to go through the line. He looks at Mr. McNamara.
"Did you really like our maple syrup, sir?"
"Yes, I loved it!" replies Mr. McNamara. "When you send down the contracts for Stephen and David, please write down your mailing address and Mr. Nicols and Gary and Tamara's to and I'll send ya's up some more from our boildown this spring which will start in twelve or thirteen days." Mr. Nicols smiles brightly, "hey that's a deal young man."
"Thanks so much!!!" God bless you, Mr. McNamara.
God bless you young man. David shakes everyone's hand and the very last person is Mr. Nicols. He is smiling widely and brightly.
"David, I'm sorry we kept you and Stephen in suspense there, and made ya's sweat. But that happens from time to time in life and especially in the NHL sir." David smiles!
"It's all good Mr. Nicols, I just am so happy and glad I get to wear a Leaf's jersey and become a Maple Leaf! God's got good things in store for you!"
"God bless you Mr. Nicols. We will talk soon! The boys make their way through security then to their gate and then wait for the big bird home!! Mr. McNamara, Mr. Nicols, Gary and Tamara walk down to the windows across from the waiting area and wave goodbye to the boys. A great bunch of kids," says Mr. McNamara, as they walk away. I think the Leafs are gonna be the best for having two of them," says Gary. "Amen, hunny," says Mrs. Gary. "They sure will," Larry smiles and says!"

Frederick Demerchant

Miracle From First Pit Pond

Chapter 12: You Can't Keep a Good man Down

As the plane touches down. There are three happy moms waiting at the airport! Mrs. Theriault, Mrs. Gardner, and Mrs. Gallagher. Brandon Copp is the first one in and he smiles, "Hello, everybody!"
"Well hello, Brandon, how are you?"Asks, Mrs. Gardner.
"Just great!" he smiles at Mrs. Theriault. "Think your son has some news for you, that you're gonna like!!"
"Mom, mom," Stephen shouts with a very loud voice as he sees his mother. "You're not gonna believe what happened!!"
"What happened?" she asks with a smile on her face. "The leafs want David and I to play for them!!!"
"Wow, I'm so happy for you guys!!" she smiles and says.
"Yep you might just see the Stanley Cup in St. Croix, NB yet Mrs. Theriault."
"Well I hope so LeRoy," she smiles and says.
"Hi, son," Mrs. Gardner says as she hugs LeRoy. "Where's that baby brother of yours?"
"I don't know, he's back there somewhere." LeRoy says in his rough gruff way. But certainly not meaning anything by it. David and Marty are the last to come in off the plane. Donna June looks at her son and smiles.
"Hi son, welcome home," as she extends her arms to him, David hugs his mom.
"Hi, mom, great to see ya!!!" Donna Junes says, "well I hear we have two Maple Leafs in the group.
"Yes mom, I can't believe it, David smiles and says!
"That's great, David!! I'm so proud of you!!" says Donna June.

"It feels like I've been away forever!" David says to his mom. As he walks over to the conveyor belt to grab his suitcase, he smiles and thinks it's great to be home. "Well did everyone get everything?" asks Peter Eales.
"I believe so," replies Stephen.
"Okay Miracles, let's go home," says Darrell Cairns.
5:00 am comes early, and David's dad was sound asleep, when David got home. But Sarah was at the kitchen table reading her Bible over a nice hot cup of tea. As her brother walked through the door, she got up quickly and ran to him and hugged him tightly.
"Hi, hi, hi!!!" David smiles and says.
"Well?" Sarah says with her big bright eyes.
"Sis, you're looking at half of the two newest members of the Toronto Maple Leafs," David smiles big and wide!!
"Oh, David, David, David, I am so happy for you!!!"
"And I assume the other half is Stephen?" she says.
"Yes, it is, sis." Donna June walks into the house and rubs David on top of his head! "How are you doing there, NHLer?" Donna June asks. David laughs and kinda tilts his head, "ohhh mom," he says.
Donna June and Saraha laugh. David and mom, I got a roast in the oven with turnips with carrots, potatoes and onions!"
"I thought I smelt something great," David smiles and says.
Sarah smiles, "would you like some?"
"That sounds wonderful, sweetheart!," replies Donna June. "I'd love some, sis!"
"It's great to be home with your's and mom's home cooking! Although I did have a wonderful, warm, toasted ham and cheese sandwich in Toronto!"
After Sarah serves her brother and mother and gets a plate for herself, David takes his mother's and sister's hand and says grace. After grace, David says, "Sarah, I want to thank you for all you've done for me."
"What do you mean, big brother?" As she sips on her tea.
"Sarah when you had your class trip to PEI that summer, had you never went, you never would have met Mr. Nicols. And had you not met him, you wouldn't have told him about me. I never would

have had a try out and never would have become a Maple Leaf, had it not been for you!"
"Oh, that's so sweet of you to say big brother!" Sarah smiles and says.
"Yes, it is," says Donna June.
As they all finish up, they say goodnight and they all turn in for the night. At 5:40 am, David goes into the barn. "Good morning Dad!!!" David smiles and says. "Good morning, son!! Great to see ya. I've missed you! And I hear congratulations are in order for you and Stephen!" David starts to clean a stall as he talks with his dad.
"Dad, my life is gonna change a lot in the next three hundred and sixty five days. But I want you to know I love you and mom very, very much. And I wanna say thank you to both of you for always loving me and providing for me, and for teaching me right from wrong."
"David, you are a wonderful son to your mother and I and we wish you all the best!"
"And we are also very, very proud of you!!!"
"I know one thing dad", David says as he continues working on the stall. "I sure am glad I'll be off from roughly June first to August fifteenth."
"Oh, really son, why is that?"
"Cause I can't wait to come home to the family farm! And see my family!!"
"Well son, a wise man once told me, always, always reach for the stars, but don't forget to remember your home!!" David smiles and looks at his dad.
"Thanks, Dad!"
"Are there two hungry guys out here?" Sarah walks in and asks.
"You better believe it sweetheart!" replies Michael.
"Well come in in if you want toasted raisin bread, bacon, scrambled eggs and homemade blackberry jam. Mom and I made it last August."
"Oh, Oh man," David smiles and says, "you don't have to tell me twice," replied David with a big smile on his face.
"Well come on in Mr. NHLer," Saraha smiles and says.

After all the family has a nice breakfast together, they pray. And David, Sarah and Kevin get ready for school. They walk out to the end of the drive and look back at their dad waving at them as they are watching the bus approach from down the road. They all wave and smile at their dad. Michael scratches his head and says, "well time to gather the eggs." As the kids all get on the bus, they all are talking about the big Toronto trip. As they get all aboard the bus from St. Croix, LeRoy Gardner, Marty Gardner, Peter Eales, Brandon Copp and Darrell Cairns.
"So do you figure you had as much fun as I did on my PEI trip?" Sarah asks LeRoy.
"Oh, Saraha it was just lovely, it really was," LeRoy replies.
"That's awesome and who would have thought we now have not one but two NHL players from little ol' rural Southwest, New Brunswick."
"Always hold to your dreams. LeRoy you never ever know, what kind of good things can come your way!"
"Amen!!" LeRoy smiles and replies to Sarah.
As the bus rolls up to the school and parks. The kids all make their way into their home rooms. When David walks in there is a student sitting around Stephen Theriault's desk talking to him. Then about eight or nine more run over to David.
Kelsey Jones, says "Hi David, how are you?" David replies. "Just great, thanks."
"Man I can't believe we are gonna be graduating with two future Toronto Maple Leafs!!!"
"Aww, thanks Kelsey!" replies David.
"But we have a long way to go yet. We have to sign our offer contracts and go to summer training camp."
"Well David, you can do it, especially with Stephen there to encourage you and you there to encourage him. Man, I'm so excited to watch you guys this fall on hockey night in Canada." Gerald Beraiult replies.
"Thanks Gerald," says David.
"I pray God will give me the strength and wisdom to be the best player I can be."
"He will be my friend!" Gerald smiles and says!

Miracle From First Pit Pond

"So Stephen did you ever imagine anything like this in your wildest dreams?" asks Helen Shaw.
"No Helen, I never did imagine anything like this, but I never would have gotten a try out had it not been for David."
"And I never would have gotten a scout to see us had it not been for my sister Sarah." says David.
"Well it just goes to show how one little event or meeting can have life changing consequences."
As the conversation is taking place, Mr. Gunter walks into the classroom pushing a TV stand holding a TV and VCR class. Please take your seats," says Mr. Gunter.
"Did anyone see the 7:00am news this morning?"
"I did Mr. Gunter," replies Helen Shaw.
"Well I was eating a bowl of cereal," says Mr. Gunter "and I watched the 7:00 am news and it said exciting news out of rural Southwest, New Brunswick coming up on CBC. So I grabbed a tape and put it in and started recording." As he slides in the tape, and the commercial for Canadian Tire gets over, the news announcer begins. "As we told you earlier we have some exciting news out of rural Southwest, New Brunswick with a Toronto Maple Leaf connection. For the first time in Toronto Maple Leafs history, not one but two players from rural Southwest New Brunswick will be on the roster for the upcoming fall winter 1988/1989 season. CBC news caught up with Mr. Gerry McNamara the general manager of the Leafs Sunday evening after their game with Boston Bruins at Maple Leaf Gardens. "
"Mr. McNamara, CBC news have learned from Tim Rushner assistant coach for the Leafs that there are definitely two young men from Southwest, New Brunswick joining the Leafs this fall/winter season sir?"
"Yes, good evening. That information is true and accurate. One will be a goalkeeper, we are sure of this. But we are not quite sure, one hundred percent sure where our other player will be. A strong possibility of right wing, but maybe perhaps the center, but we aren't exactly sure, as of yet."
"Where are the young men from, Mr. McNamara?" asks the reporter.
"Both young men are from New Brunswick, Canada."

" From a junior team in Moncton or Saint John?"
"No, that's incorrect," replies Mr. McNamara.
"Were they prospects for the Fredericton express?"
"Montreal Farm, AHL team in New Brunswick? And Toronto beat them to the punch and you negotiated a deal with them, sir?"
"No," replies Mr. McNamara. "I want to tell you that both guys were recruited from an outdoor pond in South Western, New Brunswick."
"An outdoor pond?" the reporter asks.
"Yes, that is correct Mr. McNamara smiles and says."
"Do you really think the guys can compete in the big leagues? The NHL?"
"I have no doubt of it!" Mr. McNamara smiles and says.
"Rocket Richard, Gordie Howe and lets not forget number 99 Wayne Gretzysky was homemade by his dad," says the reporter.
"That may be," says Mr. McNamara.
"But I think he did just fine in the NHL? Don't you?" Mr. McNamara smiles and says.
"Are you able to tell us any information about the young men, sir?"
"They both are from Southwest, rural NB. One makes his home in St. Croix, NB and one makes his home in McAdam, NB."
"And their team is called the St. Croix Miracles."
"Anything else, sir?" asks the reporter.
"They are both graduating high school in June."
"Sir, could we get their names and ages?"
"Yes, David Gallagher who is seventeen and Stephen Theriault who is seventeen." " Sir, where the boys are only seventeen and not eighteen is there any legal ramifications?"
"Like will their parents or a lawyer perhaps have to cosign on their contract?"
"No, this will not be an issue," replies Mr. McNamara because david turns eighteen april4th. Stephen oct8th both men will be eighteen before the offical season beginning of oct19th.Maple Leaf, NHL obligation officially begins. So they will definitely be Maple Leafs but contacts aren't drawn up yet?"

Miracle From First Pit Pond

"That's correct, but the contracts will be completed by 11:00 am Wednesday morning. Then carried to the boys homes so by Saturday morning at the very latest the contracts should be in the young men's hands."
"Mr. McNamara, thank you, sir, and goodluck with the two new prospects!" says the reporter.
"Thank you, sir and God bless!" replies Mr. McNamara. "Wow, pretty exciting breaking news out of the Southwest, New Brunswick this morning. For the first time ever in Toronto Maple Leafs history, two players will be signed at the same time from New Brunswick, Canada. And it all started from a frozen pond. For CBC news, I'm Oliver Jones reporting."
The whole classroom erupts with applause! "Congratulations David, and Stephen!" Mr. Gunter smiles and says. "Class I recorded this and brought it in cause I have four pieces of good news. The first and second bits are congratulations again to Stephen and David."
"Thank you, so much Mr. Gunter!" David replies.
"Yes, thanks a lot!!" Stephen smiles and says.
"The third bit of good news is Kalvin Palmer you will not be attending summer school this summer. As Mr. Gunter slaps Kalvin's essay down on his desk. Mr. Gunter smiles and says, "read it and weep, Kalvin! How about aloud so the whole class can hear you. Kalvin your historical and social aspects of this essay were great! Well presented and good grammar! Great job."
"Thanks Mr. Gunter!" Kalvin smiles and says.
"You're welcome Kalvin. Don't forget to tell the class your grade, eighty-eight percent."
"What, I can't believe it!!" Kalvin smiles and says.
"Yes, young man, you deserve that mark. This pushes your third quarter average up to seventy two percent. The pass mark is sixty-five percent. Nice work Kalvin!" Mr. Gunter smiles and says. "Class, I can't emphasize this enough, look at how well all of you can do when you apply yourselves! Apply yourself, apply yourself, apply yourself! Don't forget that your whole lives."
"What's the fourth bit of good news, Mr. Gunter?" asks Tammy Sloan.

"Well I was busy on Friday and I didn't catch the post office," replied Mr. Gunter. "So on Saturday morning, Mrs. Gunter and I walked down and got a letter addressed to the class of 1988. So I opened it up and read it!"

"Good, good news is here! Tammy would you like to read it to the class?"

"Sure!" Tammy smiles and says. "Well come on right up here young lady!"

Tammy comes up and Mr. Gunter hands her the letter. "Dear graduating class of 1988 of MCHS. First and foremost to each and everyone of you on your upcoming graduation congratulations! Twelve years of study has paid off! We are writing to inform you that we will not be offering a one hundred and fifty dollar cash bonus this year to the most improved student. After sixteen years of being in business in St. Croix, New Brunswick, we have decided that one hundred and fifty dollar cash bonus is no longer appropriate for most improved students of the graduating class. Therefore, we have decided to increase the most improved student cash bonus up to two hundred and sixty dollars. Plus we are doing three more one hundred dollar bonus bursaries for each student continuing their education in forestry and trades. In addition a fifty dollar cash bonus bursaries for any student in grade ten, eleven, or twelve for most sportsman or sportslady like player. For sports and a seventy five dollar cash bonus bursary for any student in grade nine, ten, eleven or twelve with a perfect attendance record. We have had one of our best fiscal financial years in 1988, thanks to our employees and contractors from the St. Croix, McAdam, Harvey Station, Magaguadavic Brockway and St. Stephen areas. So we are enclosing a check made out to MCHS 1988 graduating class for five hundred and forty dollars. Twenty dollars cash gift for each member of the graduating class! Southwest Forestry values hard work and education. And we are very proud of the twenty seven graduates for this wonderful milestone in your lives! And we say a special congratulations to Rachel Blair, Stephen Theriault, Rebecca Leblanc, David Gallagher, and Benjamin Day and Tory Norton and David Swim. Seven children of our valued employees and valued contractors. Please note, Southwest Valley

Forestry will have four student summer job openings beginning four days after graduation and running till September 1st, 1988. With the possibility of two of the jobs becoming full time. Preference will be given to the graduating class students first but we will accept applicants from grades ten and eleven if not enough apply from grade twelve. Keep reaching for your dreams and all the best in the future! And remember, showing up and determination is two thirds of the battle. Sincerely Mr. Timothy Walker, General Manager, Southwest Valley Forestry.
Mr. Gunter says, "thank you Tammy."
"Ronnie where you are class president please sign the back of the check and at lunch, I'll drive you down to the bank and could you cash it please?"
"Sure Mr. Gunter," replies Ronnie Williams, class president.
"I want you to know I'm so proud of each and everyone of you!" Mr. Gunter smiles and says. "And keep up your good hard work all the way through life!" Mr. Gunter takes roll call and all the class is present.
"Ok, now time for European history and migration to North America. Mr. Gunter starts into his lesson. Meanwhile, back at the Gallagher family farm.
"Wow, twenty-five eggs this morning!!" Donna June smiles and replies.
"Are you sure, you're not missing any from yesterday?" asks Michael to Donna June.
"No, not a one as far as I know sweetheart!" Donna June smiles and says.
"At this rate, we will not have to buy one egg for my cake business."
"By the way, how is that going hun?"asks Michael.
"Overall quite good. February fifteenth through May first is always a little slower. Valentine's day and the holidays are over. But then after May first, wedding, graduation and picnic season starts so a lot more orders will be coming." Michael pours a cold glass of milk in his right hand and puts his left arm around Donna June.
"So maybe you will have a little extra time to make me some of your wonderful peanut butter cookies!!"

Donna June gazes lovingly into her husband's eyes. "Maybe it will give me more time to kiss my husband," Donna June smiles and says.
"I like the sound of that Michael smiles and says. Donne June puckers up and gives him a big kiss on his lips! "I love you!" Donna June says.
"I love you too sweetheart," replies Michael. Just then the phone rings.
"Hello," Donna June says.
"Hey Joseph, how are you?"
"Good, good. Hey did Sarah call you up at night and tell you the good news about David?" "Yea, yea, it's all time they are gonna sign Stephen Theriault for a goalie." "And David to yes. But they're unsure of his position yet. I know it's pretty exciting!" says Donna June. "So how's everything going for you up in Ontario, sweetheart? Well that's great! That's great son. I'm very proud of you!! I love you too, Joseph. Sure, I'll put your dad right on."
"Hi son how are you?" asks Michael. "Oh great, yes we are all fine! So you are learning a lot! That's great, Joseph! You mom and I are very proud of you! Yep! Ok, son well I love you a lot call again soon! Well I'm going out to the barn to work on the tractor, planting season will be here before we know it."
"And I'm gonna make some homemade peanut butter cookies."
"Thanks, sweetheart!"
"No problem," Donna June smiles and says. Stormy, the family dog is laying on the bales of hay, when Michael walks into the barn. Stormy jumps down off the hay and walks over to see Michael with excitement. Michael pets him on the head as he walks over to get his tool box. Stormy was half border collie and half irish setter with a heart of gold. Michael grabbed a box of milk bone treats off the shelf and gave one to Stormy. "Here ya go Stormy, a nice little treat for you!" Michael turned the key of the tractor on accessorie and pulled the light switch on and set his tool box on the floor. Un huh! One side work light is blown. I better fix that. He grabs a flat and star screwdriver, and starts to sing his favorite song of all time. As he pops the bulb out of the rubber inset holder, he sings. "He's still working on me. To make me

what I ought to be. It took him just a week to make the moon and stars, the sun and the earth and Jupiter and mars. How loving and patient he must be. He's still working on me." Michael unscrews the bulb from the wires and holds it up to the light and sees the blackness in the burnt bulb. Yep, that's an easy fix. He says. Good, good! Michael walks over to the little parts room he reaches up to the shelf to grab a 40" sealed beam bulb. As he does, he feels a sharp pain in his head. Michael struggles to keep his balance for a few seconds. But luckily he sees a five gallon pail of hydraulic oil about seven feet away. He struggles to get to it. He sits down on the pail and he notices something on his face. He takes the handkerchief out of his pocket, wipes his face. He looked down at the handkerchief and noticed a lot of blood and fluid on the handkerchief. He feels one more sharp pain in his head then he collapses off the hydraulic pail onto the floor. Stormy starts barking loudly as he runs over to Michael. Donna June is inside baking peanut butter cookies with the Christian radio station 88.5 turned up enjoying some good Christian music as she bakes! But sadly because of this she can't hear Stormy barking loudly repeatedly by Michael's side. Luckily in about twenty minutes after this horrible event, their neighbour Pete MacDonald stops in to borrow a chain. As Stormy hears the noise from Pete's GMC half ton, he runs over to Pete and begins to bark loudly and more profusely. As Pete gets out, he pets stormy.
"Hi, Stormy, how are ya boy?" Stormy just barks more and louder and begins to pace back and forth from his truck to the barn. Pete has a sense come over him that something is wrong. It was a beautiful late winter or early spring day. It was around forty two degrees so luckily the man door to the barn was left open. Pete looks over at the door. Stormy runs into the door, turns, runs out then back in again. What is it Stormy? Pete makes his way to the door. He has a bad feeling that something has happened to his friend and neighbour. Pete walks over to the door, calling Michael's name. Nobody Answers. Pete goes through the door. "Hello Michael, hello are you here?" Stormy runs to the tractor barking loudly. Pete looks and sees the wires from the worklight angling from the rubber inset. Then he looks over toward the parts

room and sees two boots and legs from the knees down lying on the floor.

"Michael, Michael," he shouts out loudly as he runs over. Stormy lays down by Michael's side.

"Good boy, Stormy, good boy," Pete says as he rubs his neck quickly. Micheal collapsed on the left side of his face on the floor. So Pete can see the blood and fluid coming out of his ear.

"Michael, can you hear me? Michael!" Pete gently takes his right hand and flips it palm up. He feels for a pulse, it's quite strong, so he is relieved for that. Pete gets up and runs towards the front door of the farmhouse. He doesn't even knock, he just opens the door and runs in. Donna June is just sliding a pan of peanut butter cookies into the oven.

"Donna June, Donna June," shouts Pete, "oh, thank goodness you're here!!"

Donna June turns down the music and looks at Pete and can tell he has a look of worry on his face. "Pete, what is it?" "Call 911 immediately, Michael collapsed out in the barn."

Donna June shuts off the oven and grabs the phone.

"911 operator, this is Donna June Gallagher in St. Croix, New Brunswick. My husband collapsed in our barn."

"Ok, is he breathing?"

"I'm not sure, a friend just found him and told me to call 911."

"Ok, mame, remain calm and your civic address?"

"We are on 1620 Route 630 in St. Croix, New Brunswick. The Gallagher farm."

"Ok, mame, I am dispatching an ambulance out of McAdam right now, the ETA for arrival should be nine to ten minutes."

"Ok, thank you so much," says Donna June.

"I'll go back out to the barn right now."

"Ok, thank you Pete."

"Mame, does your husband have any allergies or known medical conditions that might have caused him to collapse?"

"No mame, nothing at all."

"Ok, well that ambulance is currently in route."

"Can I go out to my husband?"

Miracle From First Pit Pond

"Oh, sure mame. Just remember, stay calm and try to keep him warm."

"Ok, thank you."

Donna June grabbed her coat and a coat for Micheal and ran to the barn. Pete had already taken off his coat and laid it over Micheal's chest and stomach. Pete is kneeling by him, Donna June gently sets the coat on top of Pete's. "These two coats should help to keep him warm."

"For sure," Pete smiles and says very gently Pete shakes Michael's shoulders, "Michael, can you hear me?" Donna June picks up Michaels hand and rubs it, "sweetheart, can you hear Pete and I?" All of a sudden Michael starts to move and moan a little. "Pete, Pete is that you?" Michaeal asks. "Ya, ya, it's me buddy." "Hunny can you hear my voice?" Donna June asks gently. "Donna June is that you?"

"Yes, it's me sweetheart. Pete and I are right here." A tear rolls out of Donna June's eye and down her cheek. Michael fully opens his eyes, "Donna June, don't cry." Donna June rubs away her tears and says, "just rest. Just rest the ambulance is on it's way."

"Pete, Pete, what happened?"

"What all do you remember?" asks Pete.

"Well Pete all I remember is I was taking a bulb out of the rubber mount on the tractor, and I felt a quick sharp pain in my head. I looked over and saw this pail of hydraulic oil. I tried to sit down on it and that's all I remember."

"How are you feeling now?" asks Pete. "Are you woozy or lightheaded or anything? "No, no," say's Micheal, "but I am thirsty."

"I'll go get you a glass of water, sweetheart!" Donna June replies. Donna June runs into the farmhouse. "The ambulance will be here any minute," says Pete. Donna June returns quickly with a glass of ice water. Michal sits up a bit and drinks it right down. Donna June also has a damp cloth and she wiped the blood and fluid off the side of her husband's face. Pete asks him, "have you noticed a difference in anything lately?" asks Pete.

"No, not really?" says Micaeal.

"Well maybe a headache a little more often but we have been very busy on the farm, and we cut wood all winter as well. Thought it

just may be the stress of life. All of a sudden, Pete notices the sound of an ambulance siren getting closer. The ambulance is almost here, Michael," says Donna June.
"I'll run out and tell the ambulance attendant he's in the barn," says Pete.
"Good idea, Pete, thanks!" says Donna June.
"Donna, Donna June," says Micaeal.
"Yes, dear," says Donna.
"I don't want you to worry, I'm ok. I've probably just been working a little too hard." "I've seen you work eighteen hour days on this farm and hardly flinch, so don't you give me that." Michael giggles, then Donna June smiles. The ambulance roars into the door yard.
"Yes, yes mame," says Pete. "Michael is in the barn here."
"Donna June, listen to me," says Michael.
"I'll be fine, now don't you worry about fretting ok?"
"Hello, hello?" the ambulance attendant says as she comes into the barn.
"Hi, over here," Donna June replies.
"Hi, I'm Amber, I'm a paramedic with the ambulance New Brunswick."
"Hi everyone, I'm Todd, I'm also a paramedic too."
"Hello everyone," Michael smiles and says.
Todd rolls up Micaeal's left sleeve and applies a blood pressure cusp. Donna June lovingly holds Micaeal's right hand while all this is going on. "I'm gonna take your blood pressure, ok sir." Todd smiles and says.
"Sure," says Michael. Amber asks Mr. Gallagher, "can you tell me what happened?"
"I was fixing a light on the tractor and I went into the parts room to get a light bulb. I felt a quick sharp pain in my head. So I went to sit down on the hydraulic oil pail, but apparently I collapsed."
"Amber, I'm Donne June, Micaeal's wife. I also noticed he had some blood and fluid coming out of his right ear. So I took a damp cloth and wiped it off him."
"Thanks for telling me that," replied Amber.
"Blood pressure is 129 over 86."

Miracle From First Pit Pond

"'Thanks Todd," Amber says.
"Mr. Gallagher is there anything else you can tell me?" asks Amber.
"Well I feel fine, but I have been getting more headaches as of late. But I've been working hard and very busy. I just thought they might have been from the stress of life."
"Mr. Gallagher do you have any ringing in your ears or blurred vision?" Todd asks.
"No, nothing like that." Michael says.
Amber says, "Donna June."
"Yes, mame"
"After Pete found him and we called 911 he did tell me he was very thirsty so I went in the house and got him a glass of ice water and he drank it right down."
"Ok, thanks mame." All of a sudden a call comes out to Amber and Todd via their ambulance radio. Dispatch to ambulance 217, do you copy?
"Yes, go ahead," Amber replies. "What is the current situation at the Gallagher's?"
"Mr. Gallagher is conscious and talking to us his blood pressure is good. All his vital signs look good."
"Good," says the 911 operator. My medical assessment is he should be brought in for a cat scan and an MRI."
"Ok," replies the 911 operator, I'll call ahead to arrange admittance."
"Ten four," Amber replies over her radio. "Thank you, Amber," says the 911 operator.
"You're welcome," Amber replies.
"Southwest, New Brunswick dispatch, over and out."
"Ok, Mr. Gallagher, Todd's gonna get the roll bed and we are gonna load you into the ambulance and take you to the hospital in Fredericton, ok?"
"Ok," replies Micaeal.
"Donna June, why don't you go in and write a note and tell the kids where you are. I'll go to Vanceboro and gas up the car and Stephanie and I will ride in with you."
"Are you sure you don't mind Pete?" Asks Donna June.
"No, No, it's no problem at all."

Todd brings in the roll bed. Amber and Tood help Michael get in and strap him down.

"Sweetheart, Amber and Todd are gonna take you into the hospital by ambulance, Stephanie, Pete, and I won't be long behind you in their car ok?"

"Ok, dear," says Michael.

"I'm gonna go to Vanceboro to gas up," replies Pete. Stephanie and I will be down in fifteen minutes or so to get you ok?"

"Ok, Pete," thanks so much," says Donna June.

Michael gets loaded into the ambulance. Donna June writes her note. Pete goes to Vanceboro to gas up the car and the ambulance hits the road. Micaeal and Donna June have been through so much together. They both had an undying unwavering love for one another. A love pure, a love strong. A love that is so desperately precious in this world. Donna June wrote her note and twenty minutes later, Stephanie and Pete pulled into the yard in their car. Well as the school day got over all the St. Croix kids were making their way home on the bus. Sarah and David are sitting together, talking.

"Sarah, thank you so much for putting in a good world for me to Mr. Nicols, when you met him in PEI."

"You're welcome big brother. But you know your hard work and dedication to hockey helped to get the wheels in motion to you know."

"Oh, I know," says David, "but it never hurt to have someone pulling in your corner," says David.

"This is true!" Sarah giggles and smiles.

"Do you remember the time we went downhill skiing at Crabbe mountain with our youth group? You wiped out and Chandra Russell from Harvey Station Church came over and got you up and took you into the lodge and kept buying you orange crush and french friends and gravy and snuggled right into you?"

"And I came in and said Chandra, he can't have gravy, his hands will swell up and he won't be able to ski or hold the poles any more."

"Oh, no, she said, what should I do?"

Miracle From First Pit Pond

"Ha, ha, ha, ha, I remember sis," David chuckles. "You said go to the drug store and get epsom salts to soak his hands in, hurry, hurry. Ha, ha, ha, I remember sis that was kind of mean. She had a crush on me for two years."
"I know, I know, but I also knew you would wanna get back out on the slopes. I had your back, so you could!!"
"Oh man, sis God love ya!!" David smiles and says.
"Good times in the maritimes, big brother."
"You guys are funny!" Little Kevin Gallagher laughs and says!"
"And you're gonna be a heartbreaker too," Sarah smiles and says, "just like our big brother David!" Sarah pinches Kevin's cute little cheek.
"Ha, ha, ha," little Kevin Gallagher laughs. As the bus stops in front of the Gallagher farm, the kids make their way off and down the drive.
"Sarah, I want you to know I love you and David very much," says little Kevin, as they make their way up to the house.
"Well, we love you too buddy!!"
"Thanks, David." Kevin smiles and says.
"I love Joseph too! I'm glad he phones me Friday and Tuesday nights."
"He will be home before you know it, little brother." Says David.
"Now, who would like some ice cold milk and some chocolate cake I made last night for an after school snack?" Kevin and David look at each other and smile and say together, "me please." As David sees the note, he picks it up off the table and reads it. Sarah asks Kevin, " can you grab three glasses, three saucers and three forks for me please, Kevin?"
"Sure," Kevin smiles and says.
"I'll grab the cake and milk," says Sarah.
"Hey Sarah?" "Yes big brother," Sarah says.
"Mom left a note and asked me to check the water trough in the barn. I don't know if there is an issue with the intake waterline or what. But could you get all our cake and milk on the table and let Kevin start eating, then come to the barn for a second and help me?"
"Sure," says Sarah

As David opens the door to go out to the barn. "David?" Kevin says in his little voice.
"Yes Kevin?" David says, "I'll say grace for all of us and thank God for this lovely snack Sarah is getting us!"
"Okay, buddy, that sounds great!" says David. As David walks into the barn, he is pacing back and forth to the tractor. After a few minutes Sarah comes out into the barn. She opens the door and sees David pacing back and forth. "David, David, what is it?"
"Sarah, oh Sarah, I don't want to lie, but I had to get you out here alone."
"What's going on?" asks Sarah with a look of puzzlement on her face. David pulls the note out of his pocket and hands it to Sarah. Sarah begins to read it aloud. "Dear kids, I am at the Fredericton hospital with Pete and Stephanie. Your dad isn't feeling well and he's here for a test or two. I'll call you guys at 5:30 sharp. Love mom!"
Sarah gets a look of worry on her face. David reaches out and puts his arm around Sarah's shoulder. He sees a tear roll down Sarah's cheek. David wraps his other arm around her, and begins to hold her as she begins to cry. "Shh, Sarah shhh, shh Sarah. Sarahdon't cry, don't cry. Don't cry."
Now we learned earlier that Sarah Gallagher is the glue that holds the Gallagher family together, but sometimes even the strongest glue can break! Sarah genuinely loved every member of her family, but she was especially close to her dad. "Shh, shh, Sarah don't cry," David said as he held and consoled her. "What do you suppose is going on, David?" Sarah asks.
"I'm not sure," he replies, "but I think it's best if we let mom tell Kevin, don't you?"
"Yes, yes, I do," Sarah replies.
"Ok, well let's go home and have our snack that you so lovingly prepared for us." Sarah wipes away her tears. Sarah hugs David very, very tightly. "I love you big brother."
"I love you, Sarah." Sarah smiles. David looks at her and says, " Sarah?"

"Yes, David?" David replies, "Before the mountains were brought forth, or ever thou hadst formed the earth and the world, even from everlasting to everlasting, thou art God. Psalm 90:2."
"Don't worry Sarah, God has dad in his hands." Sarah smiled and said, "Thank you, David." As they walk back into the house, Sarah runs right over to Kevin, gives him a great big hug and kiss on the cheek. Kevin is sitting with his little hands folded, "Hey it's time to say grace."
"I know Kevin, but I just feel like I'm the luckiest girl in the world, wanna know why?"
"Yes, why?" Kevin looks up and asks. "Because I got three of the best brothers in the world," Sarah smiles and says. "Aww thanks sis," Kevin says. "Now let's have some cake and milk." David walks over and they all embrace.
"Hey Sarah?" "Yes, Kevin?" "Why don't you say grace?"
"I thought you said you were gonna buddy."
"I don't know why," Kevin says, "but something came over me and I think you should!"
"Sure buddy, I'd be happy to! They all join hands as Sarah begins to pray. Dear Jesus, thanks for the cake and milk we are about to receive. Thanks for the love of my brothers. And we say a special prayer as well and trust you to answer it, in your time and in your way. In Jesus' name Amen."
"Amen," says David.
"Amen," says Kevin.
"Hey Sarah?"
"Yes, Kevin?"
"Who was your special prayer for?"
"Just someone I know going through something."
"Well don't worry," replies Kevin, "God knows what he's doing!"
"Out of the mouth of babes, Ay Sarah," David replies.
Sarah looks up and smiles at David. Kevin smiles and digs right in his cake, "mmmmmmm...this is wonderful cake, Sarah!!" Kevin smiles and replies.
"I'm glad you're enjoying it pal!"
As they all sit there eating their cake, and drinking their milk, Sarah and David look up at the clock, 4:27 pm. It won't be long now and the phone will ring. After what seemed to be an eternity,

plus one. At 5:27 pm sharp, Sarah walks over to the phone. Sarah winks at David. David winks back.

"Hey, Kevin, I'm gonna run a couple of bales of hay down to the lower end of the field to make sure the cows have enough. You wanna go for a piggyback ride down with me?"

"All right!!" Kevin throws his little hands up in the air!

"We will be back in ten minutes sis!!" says David.

"Ok, I love you guys!!"

"We love you too," Kevin smiles and says. When Kevin and David get in the driveway, he heaves Kevin up on his shoulders. "Woa hooo!!!" Kevin says.

Sarah looks up at the clock, it's exactly 5:29 pm. Then she thinks it won't be long now. Donna June was always a very punctual person. About fourteen seconds go by and the phone rings.

"Hello," "Hello, hey lil sis, how are you?"

"I'm good Joseph, I'm in the middle of something very important. Can I call you right back in four or five minutes?"

"Yea, sure?" replies Joseph. "I'm just getting home from my apprenticeship program. Okay will do!"

"I love you big brother!"

"I love you to little sis! Bye, bye"

Sarah quickly hands up the phone a second till 5:30 pm. 9-8-7-6-5-4-3-2-1. 5:30 pm no call, how much longer? Sarah wonders. 5:30 pm and twenty-four seconds in comes a call.

"Hello," Sarah answers.

"Sarah, sweetheart, how are you?"

"Hi mom, I'm so glad to hear from you!! How is dad?"

"Well Sarah, he isn't too bad considering everything. But today in the barn he didn't feel well and he collapsed in the barn."

"COLLAPSED!!!" says Sarah.

"Yes, but our neighbour Pete had to borrow a chain and he found him very soon afterwards! We called 911 and your dad was conscious before they arrived. So they have run a couple tests on him today, dear."

"Tests? What tests?" asks Sarah.

"Well your dad has been having a little pain and stuff but he hasn't mentioned anything to anyone. So today, they ran an MRI test and

Miracle From First Pit Pond

ultrasound test. Tomorrow he is gonna have a head test of some sort. At 11:00 am sharp for that test. Then depending how that goes he should be able to come home."

"What do you think is maybe going on with him, mom?"

"I don't really know," says Donna June, but this is the place to find out!!"

"Well mom, I love you and dad so much!!"

"We love you too sweetheart!!"

"They brought your dad's super into him at 5:00 pm sharp. It was two scoops of mashed potatoes, green beans, butternut squash and a chicken breast. And for dessert vanilla pudding. Your dad scarfed it all down all except some of the butternut squash. But as you know, butternut squash isn't his favorite. Oh and he had a cup of tea and a glass of orange juice too."

"Well that sounds like a good sign mom!!"

"Oh yes!"

"Is Pete and Stephanie still with you?"

"Yes, they're going home in about a half an hour."

"Will you please tell them I appreciate them being good friends and neighbours to us?"

"Sure, hunny."

"I'm going to spend the night, but Pete and Stephanie said they're going to come in at 12:30 pm sharp tomorrow to pick me up and if your dad can, he will come home with us too."

All of a sudden the call is disrupted by a loud knock at the door.

"So tomorrow Sarah we all should have a more clear picture," says Donna June.

All of a sudden a loud knock again. "Mom, mom can you hold for just a second, someone is at the door."

"Sure, hunny."

"Don't hang up I'll be right back." Another knock "Coming, I'm coming," shouts Saraha. She opens the door and there is a friendly man in a purolator courier uniform.

"Hello young lady!"

"Hi," replies Sarah.

The man looks at his paperwork, "would Mr. David Gallagher be home?"

"Yes, but he's down in the field right now."

"I have a business envelope here for him."
"I can run down quickly and get him." Sarah replies.
"Miss, do you reside in this residence as well?"
"Yes."
"You don't have to run down. You can sign." Sarah signs and the friendly man hands her a big business size envelope. "Have a great weekend!"
"You too, thanks."
"You're welcome. Bye, bye."
Sarah grabs the phone, "Hi mom."
"Hi sweetie."
"Mom we haven't told Kevin anything. David and I thought maybe you should break the news to him."
"Ok, sweetheart."
"Mom we, meaning David and I are gonna pray for you and dad. I'm gonna pray God will give you strength and pray for dad too!"
"Don't forget Saraha God has us all in his hands!"
"I know mom."
"I love you Saraha, I'll call at 9:00 pm.
"Ok, I'll make sure Kevin is in bed at 8:30pm."
"I love you, Saraha."
"Love you too, mom."
"Bye, bye, dear."
"Bye, bye, mom, I love you."
As the call is disconnected, she immediately phones Joseph back.
"Hi Joseph, how are ya big bro?"
"Hi, sis, so how was your day, today?"
"Great, I'm learning a lot!"
"So how's everything there?"
"Well hectic, but what's new? Farming, hockey, church, family."
"Ha, ha, ha," laughs Joseph.
"Sarah?"
"Yes?"
"Sarah, take a big breath. Your favorite season and mine spring, officially starts in three days."
"I know, I know, I love you Joseph."
"Ha, ha ,ha, I love you kiddo. Hey is mom and dad there?"

Miracle From First Pit Pond

"No, they are in Fredericton this evening."
"Oh, okay well it's a lovely evening here, think I'm gonna go for a walk."
"Ok, Joseph, I love you!!"
"I love you too!! I'll call again soon. Oh by the way is Kevin there?"
"No he's down in the field with David."
"Oh, ok, well just tell him I love him and I'll call him Tuesday after supper. Ok I love you."
Sarah hangs up the phone and grabs three tea bags and puts the pot half full of water and sets it on a burner and turns it on. All of a sudden, the phone rings again. "Hello?" replies Sarah. She hears a familiar friendly voice. "Hi, Sarah, how are you my friend?"
"I'm okay, Stephen, and you?" "Good, thank you. Is David there?"
"No, he's down in the field."
"Oh no problem. Did he get his contract offer?"
"Well a purolator courier guy brought a big business envelope for him."
"Yep, that's it!"
"Oh, he will be happy for that!" replies Sarah. "Just tell him to call me later. Have a great evening Sarah."
"You too, Stephen, bye, bye."
"Bye Sarah." As the teapot begins to whistle Saraha grabs two tea cups and pours. The door swings open. "Duck your head down, buddy!"
"Ok, big brother!!!"
"Sarah the cows won't go hungry, we fed them!" Kevin smiles and says.
"Good job buddy," replies Sarah. David sets Kevin on the floor.
"Hey, David, I made some tea. Two sugar black she asks?"
"Oh, yeah sis, thanks." She gives David his tea. David says, "Kevin do you have any homework?"
"Yes, I got reading and spelling."
"Ok, buddy, you take it up to your room and do it?"
"Yep, love you guys" Kevin smiles and says.
"We love you too buddy," Sarah smiles and says.
"You better believe it!" says David.
"Hey Kevin?"

"Yes, Sarah."
"Joseph phoned and said he loved you and he will call you Tuesday evening."
"Alright!" Kevin smiles and says as he goes upstairs.
"Oh, David, a business envelope came for you from a purolator courier."
"Oh, thanks sis. Did you tell Joseph what happened?"
"No, I didn't," replies Sarah.
"Well what all did mom say?"
"Well dad had some sort of spell in the barn today. He collapsed and they had to call the ambulance."
"What!!?" says David.
"Yeah, luckily Pete MacDonald found him shortly after it happened and they called 911!"
"Well, what's wrong?"
"They don't know yet, mom said he had two tests today and one more tomorrow, but if it all goes good, he can come home tomorrow."
"Sarah what do you think it may be?"
"I'm not sure. But let's pray."
"Ok, David smiles and says as he holds Sarah's hand. "Dear Jesus, we think of mom and dad, please be with them both. Guide the doctor's hands and minds to figure out what's going on with dad please. Thanks for your love. In Jesus name, Amen."
"Amen, oh Stephen wants you to give him a call to."
"Ok, thanks sis," as Sarah goes into the living room with her tea. David phones Stephen. "Hello Stephen."
"Hello," Stephen's friendly voice says.
"Hi, pal, how are ya?"
"I'm ok," says David. "Dad is in the hospital."
"Ya apparently he had some sort of spell. Ya they're running tests on him," says David.
"Yep, I got it."
"Oh, it is our contracts?"
"Well, thanks," says David.
"I was very very happy with my offer David," replies Stephen.

"Mom and dad read it and said it sounds great." They're signing me for two years."
"What does yours say?"
"I haven't opened it yet buddy," says David.
"Well I'm sure it will be a great one," replied Stephen.
"Thanks buddy."
"David, I'll pray for you and your dad!"
"Thanks, Stephen.I just wanna find out what's going on."
"Well have a good evening, my friend, we will talk soon."
"Goodnight Stephen."
"Night, pal."
David takes his Bible and lays on his bed and begins to read. He turns to where he left off Psalms 20:4. David goes to flip on his side, but he accidentally knocks his Bible on the floor. It landed pages down. When he picks it up, he notices it was in James. David looks up to his ceiling and smiles and says, "Ok, Lord what are you trying to tell me here?" He begins to read James chapter 5 where it landed. When he gets to verses 15 and 16 he reads. And the prayer of faith shall save the sick, and the Lord shall raise him up, and if he has committed sins, they shall be forgiven him. Confess your faults one to another, and pray one for another, that ye may be healed. The effectual fervent prayer of a righteous man availeth much. David has a great peace come over him. The peace that passes all understanding. David shuts his Bible and puts it on his night table. "Dear Lord, I know you're with dad tonight, please help him. And heal him or whatever is wrong. Thanks for all you do for us everyday! In Jesus name, Amen." David shuts his eyes and falls asleep.

****

The sun is shining brightly at 10:45 am in Fredericton, New Brunswick. Donna June is sipping on a coffee and holding Micheals hand. "How are you feeling, sweetheart?" Asks Donna June.
"Good. Breakfast was good, I don't think I have had raisin bran for over a year now. And the toast was good, but I got a confession, not as good as your homemade bread. Donna June smiles and strokes Micheals hair.
"Hello, good morning," a friendly nurse says.

"Hi," replies Micheal.
"Hello," Donna June smiles and says.
Mr. Gallagher I'm Mona, good morning."
"Good morning, Mona."
"We are gonna get you up. Set ya in a wheelchair. Wheel ya down to the elevators then down to the second floor for your test ok?"
"Ok. sure."
As Micheal gets off the elevator, Mona is wheeling him and Donna June is by her side. They take him into a room with a square looking machine with a lot of wires.
"There ya go," Mona smiles and says, "Doctor McKinely is your doctor and he will be here in a minute or two.
"Hope this test goes well."Micheal looks up at Donna June and says.
Donna June smiles and says, "it will sweetheart." Donna June looks at the wall clock 10:57 am "it won't be long now dear." Back at the farm in St. Croix as the clock chimes 10:58 am the phone rings. David answers it.
"Hello."
"Hello David, how are you?"
"I'm good thanks."
"David, its pastor Roach calling. Listen we just heard about our dad. Is he home?"
"No, he is in the hospital. He has one more test today, but if it goes good he can come home."
"Oh, good, good," replies pastor Roach.
"Well we are praying for you all and we love you all!"
"We love you too, pastor."
"Thanks for praying."
"It's my pleasure. When your dad gets home and feels up to it, tell him to give me a call ok. Have a good day David!"
"You too pastor! Bye, bye, bye."

As the clock chimes 10:59 in Fredericton, New Brunswick, a middle aged doctor with curly, curly blond hair walks into the room. "Good morning everyone," he smiles and says.

Miracle From First Pit Pond

"Good morning, I'm Michael Gallagher." Michael extends his hand.
"Hi Michael, I'm doctor Paul McKinely." Donna June smiles and sticks out her hand. "Hi, I'm Donna June, Michael's wife."
"Donna June," doctor Paul McKinely says.
"Yep," replies Donna June.
"What a very beautiful name." Michael smiles, "she's just as beautiful on the inside too Dr. McKinely."
"Aww you guys." Donna June blushes and says. Michael and doctor McKinely giggle.
"Michael, I have been going over your charts and paperwork and I noticed you have been getting headaches more frequently?"
"Yes, but I thought it was just from the stresses of a life doctor."
"Well stress can cause headaches sometimes."
"But that's why I want to run this test today. What this machine tells us about the blood flow throughout your head."
"My blood pressure?" asks Michael.
"No, not your blood pressure, your blood flow. There is a difference. See blood pressure tells the pressure of your moving blood and as you know, your blood is always circulating in your body. But this machine will measure flow, and is it struggling to flow in a certain area of your head?"
"Oh, ok," replies Michael.
"Michael, since you collapsed yesterday, have you had any other headaches or pain in your body anywhere?"
"No, no sir, none."
"Ok, and no dizziness or blurred vision you said."
"Nope."
"Great. Great!!" says Dr. And no medication for anything?"
"Nope, just an aspirin once in a while."
"Ok, replies Dr. McKinely. "And no allergies."
"Yes sir, that's right," says Michael.
"Ok, Michael just sit here, relax and I'll place these wires on your head. The test will take about twenty five to thirty minutes."
"Ok," replies Michael.
"Would you like a magazine or anything to read?"
"No, that's ok, but I do have a couple questions."
"Could I ask you them after the test?"

"Sure." Dr. McKinley says.
"Ok Michael, what are your questions."
"Well I was wondering my first question is do you or the other doctors have any idea what could be going on with me yet?"
"Well we're not one hundred percent sure yet, Michael but this test will tell us a lot!! And also at 8:00 am on Monday Dr. Michelle Kenderson will be here at our hospital. She is one of the best doctors in the maritimes for blood flow. I have no surgeries scheduled Monday so Dr. Kenderson has agreed to meet with me to talk about your case. She practices out of Halifax, Nova Scotia. So by 4:45 pm Monday we should know a lot more!"
"Great," Michael smiles and says.
"Anymore, questions Michael?"
"Just two more doctors. First one, can I go home today?"
"Oh absolutely," Dr. McKinley smiles and says. "I'll be signing your release paper shortly."
"Ok, my last question is, what all can I do?"
"What all can you do?" Dr. McKinley looks puzzled.
"Well we have a family farm. I have chickens, cows, jersey and holsteins I take care of."
"Michael does your family help with the farm?"
"Yes, every single member of my family. Well but Joseph, he usually does, but he is currently in Ontario on a welding apprenticeship program."
"Oh, that's great!" Dr. McKinley smiles and says.
"Ya, he's my oldest son!"
"Well, just carry on as normal. But if you feel a headache coming on, I want you to stop and just rest for a few minutes ok?"
"Ok. Dr. McKinley, thank you so much!!"
"My pleasure!" Dr. McKinley smiles and says. Dr. McKinley is unhooking all the wires off of Michael's head. As he removes the last one, he says, "ok Michael just one more thing.
"What's that doctor McKinley?" asks Michael.
"I'm going to sign your release papers now. But on your administration admittance papers you said your weight is maintained around 200 lbs."
"Yea," says Michael, "200, 201, that area."

Miracle From First Pit Pond

"Ok, well I'm leaving the room. Shutting the door I want you to strip down to your underwear and when I come back I'll weigh you and then you're good to go. I'm going to sign your release papers, see ya in a couple minutes," says Doctor McKinley." As Dr. Mckinley exits the room. Donna June says to Michael, as he is getting undressed, "well sweetheart, that wasn't too bad."
"No, not bad at all," says Michael.
"Dr. McKinely seems very nice."
"Oh, for sure!" Michael smiles and says.
"You said Pete and Stephanie's picking us up sweetheart?"
"Yes, dear." says Donna June.
"Awesome." Dr. McKinley comes back into the room. "Ok, your paperwork is all in order."
"Ok, I'll set this scale to zero."
"Ok, Michael, get on the scale and once you do, hold still for ten second ok?"
"Sure, Dr. McKinley," replies Michael.
"Let me see, get my pen here."
"Ok, Michael when is the last time you have weighed yourself?"
"Umm, oh boy Dr. McKinley, I'm not sure, I bet it's gotta be at least eight or nine months. One summer night before I got in the shower last summer was when I did it last."
"Well, you're normally around 200 or 201 lbs?"
"Yes, why are you 192 right now. Michael step off the scale for one minute will you please."
"Ok, doctor."
"Ok, try again, now remember nice and still for ten seconds. Yep no this is accurate, 192 lbs and 3oz."
"We worked hard all winter and cut a lot of wood."
"No problem Michael, it's only eight or nine pounds but I like to be throughout.
"I'm going on my twenty third year of being a medical doctor this spring and if I've learned anything in twenty three years, I've learned the more throughout you can be, the better."
"I appreciate that Dr. McKinley."
"My pleasure."
"Well like I said, Monday Dr. Kenderson will discuss a few things and we will be in touch! Monday late afternoon at the latest."

"Thank you Dr. McKinley, God bless you!"
"God bless you folks too."
"Goodbye for now."
"Bye, bye Dr. McKinley. Thank you so much," replies Donna June.
"You're welcome."
"Donna June is such a great name," Dr. McKinley says as he walks out the door. Micheal gets dressed and by the door of his room, Stephanie and Pete are waiting for them. They load Michael's overnight bag in the car and head for home. As they leave McAdam and are almost home. Donna June says, "Pete and Stephanie what are you doing tomorrow night for supper?"
"I don't think we have any plans for supper, do we dear?" Pere asks Stephanie.
"No, why?"
"Well Michael and I would love it if you guys come down and have supper with the kids."
"Well, we would love to," replied Stephanie.
"It's a way of saying thank you for being such good friends and neighbours, and for all the kindness you've shown Michael and I," says Donna June.
"Aww shucks," says Pete.
"We ain't done much. We're just so glad they're figuring things out for Michael."
"Oh yeah, we will get 'er," says Michael.
As they finish driving and talking Stephanie and Pete pull into Michael and Donna June's yard.
"Thanks so much for everything guys!" says Michael standing by Pete's driver's door one arm holding his overnight bag the other arm around Donna June. "5:00pm tomorrow night work for yas?"
"Yup"
"Michael, listen you need any help with anything just call us ok?" Michael looks at the door of his home. David, Sarah and little Kevin are standing there anxiously waiting. "I will, but it looks like my three helpers are waiting for me!"
"Well don't forget ok?"

Miracle From First Pit Pond

"Ok" Michael removes his arm from around Donna June and shakes Pete's hand. "Thanks again for everything. God bless you guys."
"Thanks," says Pete.
"See yas at 5:00 pm tomorrow." As Stephanie and Pete back out of the yard. Sarah runs to her dad and wraps both arms around his neck. "Well hello, young lady," Michael smiles and says. Kevin runs to Donna June and jumps in her arms. "Hi, awww."
"Hi Kevin!"
"Where were you guys?"
"In Fredericton," says Donna June. "Well we all missed yas." David walks over with his hands in his jeans pockets. "Get over here," Michael smiles and says as he rubs David on top of the head. "Hey dad!"
"Hi, son!"
"Hope you guys are hungry. Sarah made us all some great tuna fish sandwiches!!"
"Sounds great son!"
The remaining snow on the ground of Southwest New Brunswick would have melted in thirty seconds if you could release the warmth of the love they all shared for one another. As they go in and have a nice lunch and some laughs. Donna June says, "well what all needs done in the barn?"
"The eggs are all gathered," replied Sarah. "David and I cleaned the stalls after breakfast.
"Well I know one thing that needs done in that barn."
"What's that sweetheart?" asks Donna June.
"I gotta finish changing that 4011 bulb."
"Hey dad?"
"Yes, son?" Michael says to David.
"Why don't you rest and I'll change that light out for ya." Michael gets up from the table, grabs his old baseball cap and throws it on his head. "Nope, I got it son. And after that I'm gonna walk another bail of hay down to the lower field for the cows."
"Ok, dad I don't mind."
"I know you don't son, and thank you." But you can't keep a good man down! No you sure can't. You can't keep a good man down.

Frederick Demerchant

Chapter 13: With a Phone call, Life can Change

At 3:00 pm that beautiful Saturday after David and his dad retorqued all the wheels on their farm tractor, David says, "Dad, my contract offer came last night."
"Oh, great," replies Michael. "Are you happy with it?"
"Yes, well to be honest I have opened it yet."
"What!? You haven't opened it yet?"
"No dad."
"Why, not?"
"Because dad you are way, way, way more important than some contract offer to play hockey."
"Aww son I love you so much!!"
"I love you to dad, but I'll tell ya what I'm dying to see what it says."
"Run in and grab it will ya?"
"Bring it out and we will read it over!!"
"Ok, dad." David smiles and says. As David goes in and grabs the purolator courier business envelope off the counter Donna June is peeling some potatoes.
"David, hey David."
"Yeah mom, it's 3:05 pm you and your dad come in by 4:00 pm please. Paul and Stephanie are gonna be here at 5:00 pm sharp to have supper with us ok?
"Ok mom. I love you."
"Donna June looks at him and smiles. "I love you too, Mr. NHLer."
"Aww, mom." David blushes. Donna June smiles. As David walks back to the barn with his business envelope in hand. His mind

wanders about a few things when will dad's test results be in? What does this contract say? Stephen was happy with his, will I think mine is fair? As he opens the barn man door, his mind automatically just goes to one thing. Well two things.
"Alright, son!! "I'm so excited to look at this!!"
His dad! The second thing, his dad's smile.
"Crack that envelope open son!! I'm so, so happy and excited for you."
"Aww, thanks dad," David says, "do you want me to read it to you dad?"
"Sure."

Dear Mr. David Gallagher. This is an official contract offer from the Toronto Maple Leafs franchise LTd. to David Michael Gallagher. Enclosed is all full contract details. For each and every thing offered. But the bullet points are listed on their first three pages.
Number one: David Michael Gallagher is offered a full four season contract offer. "Wow dad, four years!!" Micheal rubs the top of David's head.
"I'm so proud of you son!! Keep going, what else.?"
"There's more here under article one dad."
"Ok, son."
David Michael Gallagher cannot and will not be traded or choose to be a full round or partial round draft pick. He is locked to the Maple Leafs for four years exclusively. After four years David Michael Gallagher can negotiate his own trade or can be approached or offered to other teams. But the Maple Leafs can offer and renegotiate a legal deal to David for a longer term and a new contract.
"Dad, dad that sounds awesome!"
"They really believe in you David!!"
"Ya, tell me about it. Stephen only got a two year contract!!"
David shall be paid the following wage. First year: $103,000.
"Wow dad, 103,000 dollars" To be paid out on a weekly stipend pay check. David's weekly paycheck for fifty-two weeks a year will be $1980.77. All taxes will be deducted from Maple Leafs

payroll for such things as with any Canadian job income tax, Canada Pension Plan, and so on and so forth. Second season David will receive a nine percent pay raise on his overall gross first year seasonal pay. His pay will be $112,270 per year gross. David's third year salary will be $210,000 gross and his fourth year $262,000.
"Dad, dad, can you believe it? Over $262,000 for one year!"
David Michael Gallagher's four year total money to be paid to him will be.
Michael butts in very quickly, "over $685,000 if my math is correct son."
"You're good dad!!"
The grand total is $687,270.
"Not bad for an under twenty three years old son!"
"I guess not!"
Article two: All endorsement offers such as sports protective gear, shoes, restaurants and so on and so forth, should any endorsements be offered to David, are solely the responsibility of David to negotiate. Should he want to and choose to accept any, some or all offers.
"That sounds good dad!"
"Ya, not bad at all son!"
David may wear some or all Maple Leaf apparel for any, some or all offers. Such things as a jersey, baseball cap, etc, etc.
Article three: David is expected to act and display integrity and character at all times. David is to hold to Maple Leaf values when conducting interviews, making guest appearances at places, etc, etc.
Article four: Should David be hurt or injured, his full pay amounts are locked in and shall be paid to him. Any therapy or doctors appointments that David has set up for him by Maple Leafs staff or trainers David is expected to attend.
Article five: David must attend all practices whether home or out on the road. As all Maple Leaf players are expected to do.
Article six: Regardless of any and all things going on with the team. June 29th to August second is the official vacation time, time off of any and all players. There will be no team obligations of any

kind or any sort during this time period. This is over four full weeks of vacation per year to all players!

"Wow dad, when I come home, I can stay for over a month!"

"Ya, it's great son!! Hey I think everything is sounding great and fair so far! How about you?"

"It's great dad!"

Article seven: Even though it isn't legally binding we hope all players will keep a good healthy lifestyle for late summer training camp. Walking, running, jogging, swimming, canoeing, gym memberships, push ups, sit ups are some forms of summer activities or exercises to help stay healthy and fit.

Article eight: When on the road all hotels, meals, transportation to and from opposing team's city baggage fees at airports etc, etc will be paid in full and taken care of by the Toronto Maple Leafs franchise Ltd.

Article nine: There is zero tolerance when away playing opposing teams for drugs and alcohol. Any player caught consuming drugs or alcohol will be dealt with the following way. First offence written warning. Number one two game suspension fine of two thousand dollars.

"Wow dad, they take it seriously!"

"Yes as well they should."

Second offense, three week suspension without pay, thirty thousand dollar fine. Third offense termination from Maple Leafs and termination of contract effective immediately.

"Dad, I'm so happy and glad I don't drink, smoke or take drugs, it just causes so many problems!"

"Yes son, it sure does! I'm glad Jesus kept you away from those things!"

"Me, too Dad!" David smiles and says.

When a player is home if he wants a social drink at home ex: a glass of wine with a meal, a can of beer at a barbeque, that is fine. But again we stress any and all players regardless of position, title or length of years with theme or popularity with fans, if you show up to practice at home in Toronto with any indication of drug or alcohol in your body, or on your person, all penalties will apply as per rules to out on the road. Wherefore we hope and expect all

players to lead and strive for a good healthy life, mentally, emotionally, spiritually, physically, etc, etc. Any player that feels he has a drug or alcohol problem will by no means be released from the team, benched from play, fined or suspended, be little or retiqued by management. But every measure will be taken, to get the player help. This may be but not limited to, drug/alcohol rehab facility, counselling, a mentor for accountability etc, etc. All costs related to any and all of this will be covered by the Toronto Maple Leafs franchise Ltd.
Article ten: All players will be given seventeen tickets for regular season games per year at home. And five tickets per year for playoff games at home if the Maple Leafs are in the playoffs. Any other tickets needed or wanted will have to be purchased by players for regular prices.
Article eleven: All contracts will be honoured in full as they are typed up and offered to each individual player. We tell all players feel free to take contracts to a lawyer for legal advice. But the contracts will be fully honoured as typed and a lawyer is not necessary but we leave that up to the players discretion.
Welcome David Micheal Gallagher to the Toronto Maple Leafs. Sincerely, Mr. Gerry McNamara and the Toronto Maple Leafs Franchise Ltd.

"Well what do you think dad?"
"Well it seems pretty forward to me. What do you think of it David?"
"Well it sounds great!"
"As long as you're happy that's all that matters."
"Dad, thanks for all you've taught me!!"
"You're welcome son! I love you!!"
"I love you dad!!!"
"We better get in and get cleaned up for supper before Stephanie and Pete get here."
"Sounds great son!"
After a great meal of pork chops, mashed potatoes and gravy, banana cream pie, green beans and salad. And an evening of talking and laughing in the living room, Stephanie and Pete get up

and say, "thanks guys for such a lovely night!!!" "It went by so fast, I can't believe it's 8:50 pm already!!"

"Guys it was a lot of fun!" replies Donna June.

"Come down again soon," says Michael.

"We will and you guys pop up when ya's can. Michael don't forget," says Pete, "you and Donna June need anything, anything at all, just shout!"

"I will, thanks guys for being such wonderful friends and neighbours!!"

"It's our pleasure," says Stephanie.

"Thank you," says Donna June. "Goodnight," says Donna June.

"Goodnight," says Pete and Stephanie.

"Mom thanks so much for such a lovely meal," says Sarah."

"You're welcome, sweetheart."

"Mom," Kevin smiles and says, "Sarah and I talked about it, she's gonna wash and I'm gonna dry then I'm saying my prayers and going to bed cause I got Sunday School in the morning!"

"Well thank you to you and Sarah Kevin, that's very kind of you guys."

David goes up to his room and picks up his telephone. "Hi, buddy how are you?" David says as Stephen answers the phone.

"Great," replies Stephen.

"Dad and I read my contract today."

"What did you think of it?" asks Stephen.

"It's good. They offered me a four year contract."

"That's awesome buddy!"

"Thanks." David smiles and says.

"Mine is a two year contract," says Stephen. "I don't know if I mentioned that to you before or not," says Stephen. "Hey David, what do you think they will do at the end of my contract?"

"What do you mean buddy?" asks David.

"Well do you think, I'll be offered another one? Will I become a free agent? What do you think will happen?"

"Well two years is a long time, I think a lot of it will depend on what the franchise is doing, their standing in their division. A lot of different things. But you know what buddy?"

"What's that?" asks Stephen.

"All we can do is take it a day at a time."
"I'm gonna do just that," replies Stephen. "I'm gonna read my Bible and go to sleep. I'll see ya at church tomorrow buddy!"
"I look forward to it Stephen!"
"Goodnight my friend."
David grabs his Bible and picks up where he left off. Hebrews Chapter 11:3 "Through faith we understand that the worlds were framed by the word of God, so that things which are seen were not made of things which do appear." Hmm that's good David thinks to himself. All of a sudden the phone rings. David chuckles to himself. Stephen was so excited he must have forgotten to tell me something and he's calling back. It rings a second time. David picks it up. "Hello."
"Hello, I'm sorry to call at such a late hour, but this is doctor McKinley from the Doctor Everett Chalmers Hospital. Would Michael be there?"
"Sure just one second."
"Ok," replies Dr. McKinley. David gets up, walks two doors down and gently knocks on his mom and dad's bedroom door.
"Dad, Dad, are you still awake?" David says with a gentle voice.
"Your mom and I are still awake, come on in son." David opens the door.
"Dad, there's a phone call for you, the man said his name is Dr. McKinley."
"Ok, thanks son."
David goes back to his room hands up the phone and continues to read in Hebrews.
"Hello," says Michael.
"Hello Michael, I'm sorry to disturb you at such a late hour, but it's very important. It's doctor McKinley."
"No problem Dr. McKinley how are you?"
"I'm ok, thank you. I was in the hospital tonight catching up on some paperwork and I noticed your MRI results came in. I opened them up and it confirmed what I was suspicious of."
"Well what were you suspicious of Dr. McKinely?"
"Well do you remember how I weighed you and you had lost nine pounds or so?"
"Yes I remember Dr. McKinley," says Michael.

"Well you told me how you worked hard all winter logging and working on the farm. But when you hadn't weighed yourself in eight or nine months I wanted so desperately to see your MRI results. Now do you remember the test I administered the last one on blood flow pressure. Dr. Kenderson as I told you will review that with me at 8:05 am on Monday."

"Ok Dr. McKinley," replies Michael.

"But what I've been suspicious of is confirmed by your MRI, regardless of the blood flow results test. I feel God has a hand in all of this. Dr. Kenderson is an extremely busy doctor and an expert in her field. It's great she's gonna be here Monday. I'm sorry Michael, I'm rambling, please forgive me."

"It's fine Dr. Mckinley, I'm glad you believe in God as I do."

"That's great Michael!" replies Dr. McKinley.

"But Michael we are lucky, you have a mass or tumour about a third of an inch up off where your brain connects with your right ear canal. That's why there was blood and fluid that came out your ear, when your wife found you in your barn. We are lucky because in all my years of medical practice these tumours tend to be extremely aggressive and grow fast."

"Grow fast?" asks Michael.

"Yes the tumour or mass is malignant which means it's cancerous. The sooner these things are found. diagnosed, and treated the better!"

"Now do you remember how I told you I have no surgeries scheduled for Monday?"

"Yes, Dr. McKinely," replies Michael.

"Well I do now. We are gonna operate to remove the mass at 11:30 am sharp. We would like you to arrive at the hospital at 9:15 am sharp, register and tell the register you are here for surgery prep."

"Ok, Dr. McKinley."

"Michael, Dr. Kenderson is an expert in this field. She has agreed already to perform the removal surgery with me. As I said, I think God is in play here."

"Dr. McKinley?"

"Yes Michael?"

"What do you think the chances are of everything going ok in the surgery?"
"I'd say eighty percent Michael with stuff like this time is critical. Now what I want you to do is try not to worry. Carry on with your daily farm chores and know you're in good hands."
"Ok, thank you Dr. McKinley."
"Michael," says Dr. McKinley.
"Yes," replies Michael. "Can I say a prayer with you?"
"I'd be honoured."
"Heavenly Father, help ease Micheal's mind of his upcoming surgery. Guide our hands as we operate. Heal him strong and well we ask all this in Jesus' name. Amen."
"In Jesus' name, Amen." says Micheal.
"Thank you Dr. McKinley."
"You're welcome. Now don't you worry and we will see you Monday. Goodnight."
"Goodnight."
"Hunny, what did Dr.McKinley say?" asks Donna June.
"Donna June, the MRI test is in and it's confirmed what doctor McKinley thought."
"What did he think?"
"I have a malignant tumour on my brain."
"Cancer?" asks Donna June?
"Yes, sweetheart," replies Michael.
Sarah and Kevin begin to start up the stairs of their farmhouse. Donna June begins to cry very loudly and very profusely. David hears this and he rushes into his mom and dad's room.
"Mom, mom, what's wrong?"
"Oh, David, David your dad, your dad has cancer!"
David jumps up on the bed between them behind their heads.
"Oh mom, don't cry, don't cry."
Sarah and Kevin rush upstairs. When they arrive, David is half on the bed half on the floor with one arm around his mom and one around his dad. Michael has both arms around Donna June.
"Mom, mom what's wrong?"
"Oh Sarah, Sarah your dad has cancer."
Kevin begins to cry very loudly. "Does this mean daddy is sick?"
Sarah holds Kevin in one arm on her lap and rubs her mother's arm

with her free arm. "Yes, hunny," says Donna June to Kevin, "daddy is sick."
Sarah holds her head and cries. Sarah lets go of Kevin and runs over to her dad. And wraps both arms around his neck and cries and cries. Kevin is in the arms of his mother crying. Now Michael begins to cry. "Don't cry, don't cry," David just keeps repeating to everyone. And the tears fall from David's eyes down his cheeks onto the bedding for about forty five minutes. The Gallaghers just hold each other and cry. After about forty five minutes, Michael rubs his eyes and says, "family, family, give me your hands."
"What for?" asks Sarah.
"Because, we are gonna pray, then go to bed for we have church tomorrow, ya know!" says Michael. They all joined hands, "Dear Lord, you said you would never leave us or forsake us. I know you are here with us at this very moment. Please put the family's mind at ease and let them know you control all!! We ask this in Jesus name, Amen!"
"Amen," the family all says.
"Kevin, Kevin?"
"Yes, daddy."
"Come here buddy. I want you to know something important."
"What's that?" asks Kevin.
"Did you ever learn in Sunday school about a man that was sick and couldn't walk?"
"No, what happened to him daddy?"
"Well the Bible says that an angel was sent down from Heaven to stir up the water and whoever was the first to get into the water was healed and placed all better. Well one day Jesus walked by and saw a man who couldn't walk. He knew the angel was gonna come to stir up the water. So Jesus said, ``Would you like to be healed? He said every time I try to go to the water, somebody beats me there and I am not healed. So Jesus looked at him right at that moment in time and said. Be healed so Jesus looked at him right at that moment in time and said. Be healed right now, take up your mat and walk. And guess what Kevin?"
"What daddy."

Miracle From First Pit Pond

"Right at that moment in time, the man took up his mat and began to walk. Jesus healed him. Well I have Jesus. And I bet he's gonna heal me too!"
"I hope so daddy! It makes us sad when you are sick."
"Well you and mama and David and Sarah pray for me everyday and just watch what good things Jesus does!! Ok buddy!"
"Ok, daddy."
"Now go get in bed and mom and I will be in in a minute to tuck you in. Sarah hugs her dad, "I love you."
"Love you too, night mom!"
"Goodnight." David hugs his dad.
"Don't worry," replies Michael.
"Night, dad." David hugs his mom, "I love you mom."
"I love you too, sweetheart." Donna June and Michael tuck Kevin in, go back to bed, hold each other and fall asleep.
As the family drives into church the next morning Sarah asks her dad a question. "Hey dad."
"Yes, dear." replies Michael. "I just thought of something."
"Oh, what would that be?" asks Michael.
"Nobody has told Joseph anything yet have they?"
"No, they haven't" replies Michael.
"Your mom and I were lying in bed talking about it this morning. What do you think we should do? We don't wanna see him fret and worry no matter how far away he is."
"Dad can I say something?"
"Sure David," replies Michael.
"I wouldn't care how far away I was, I'd definitely wanna know if my dad was sick!!!"
"Me too dad," replies Sarah.
"I wouldn't care if I was on the moon, I'd wanna know if my mama or daddy was sick," says little Kevin.
"Well then it's settled after church we will call Joseph and tell him ok everyone."
"Ok," they all reply.
As the family makes their way into the church, Pastor Roach greets the family, "Hello Gallaghers so nice to see you all."
"Hi pastor," they all say.

The children go down to Sunday School Michael and Donna ask Pastor Roach if they can see him for a moment in his office.
"Pastor thanks for letting us see you in your office for a minute. Pastor I found out last night I have a cancerous tumour on my brain. They're gonna operate on me tomorrow morning."
"I will pray and have the church pray for Michael. During the service would you like to come forward and have some of the men of the church come forwards and pray for you?"
"Pastor we would love that."
After pastor Roach's sermon, he informs the church that Michael has cancer and is gonna be facing a surgery tomorrow. Michael comes forward to the altar and some of the men of the church come forward and lay hands on him and pray for him. Michael feels so much better in his body and spirit after this happens. The family returns home and has a nice Sunday lunch of grilled cheese sandwiches and homemade chocolate chip cookies for dessert. After their lunch, the family all gather in the living room and every member says hello to Joseph. When Michael is put on the phone with his oldest child Michael asks him he says, "Joseph are you standing up or sitting down right now?"
"I'm sitting down dad, why?"
"Well Joseph there's no easy way to say this so I'm just gonna come out and tell you. Joseph I have cancer in my brain."
"Ohhh, no dad I'm so sorry."
"It's ok Joseph, the pastor announced it at church this morning and some men came forward when I went up to the altar and prayed for me!!"
"Dad, that's great. What are your treatment options?"
"I am not one hundred percent sure but I do get operated on late tomorrow morning to remove the cancerous tumour."
"Dad, I'll see if I can get a flight out tonight to get home."
"Joseph, that's not necessary. Your course will be done before long. Mom and Saraha and Pete and Stephanie are gonna be there with me."
"Are you sure dad? I mean an operation on your brain, very, very, serious."

"I know son, but why don't you stay and finish up, but pray for me."
"I will dad, I love you and the family very, very, much."
"We love you too, son!!!"
"Please have mom call me at suppertime with an update, please dad!"
"I will son!"
"They found this very quickly. My doctor's name is Dr. McKinley. He has a colleague from Halifax who is an expert in her field name Dr. Kenderson, so don't you worry I'm in good hands!!!"
"I love you dad." The family all says in unison when their dad motions his hand the third time.
"We love you Joseph!"
"I love you too guys!!"
"Bye, bye, son!"
"Bye, bye."
The family has an afternoon of laughs and they all turn in early cause it's a big day tomorrow.

The next morning David and Kevin are out by the road waiting for the school bus to come, "I said an extra special prayer for daddy this morning, as soon as I woke up this morning. I said it!"
"That's awesome Kevin!" David smiles and says. Don't ever forget as you go through life that Jesus is, always listening! "I'm glad he does!"
"Me too buddy." Sarah walks out onto the front porch drinking her morning cup of tea. The bus stops and the boys look back. Sarah smiles and waves. The boys wave back. The boys get on and make their way to school. Sarah sat down on the deacon's bench on her front porch. She thinks to herself it's a big day today. I know God hears our prayers. I know he will be with dad during the surgery. And I know God will guide the doctors' hands and minds. I am hoping all goes good. As Sarah thinks these things out comes her dad. "Got room for one more on that bench?" He smiles and asks.
"Always dad!!" Sarah smiles and says as she looks up.
"Honey I don't want you to worry today."
Sarah looks over at her dad.
"Dad that's way easier said than done in a situation like this."

Her dad sits down beside her.
"Not really honey. I'm forty-two, I'm strong, all my vital signs are good. But if for some reason something did go wrong, I know once I leave this world I am going to Heaven. Where I will be with God forever and forever!"
"But dad if that were to happen what about mom, what about Kevin?"
"What do you mean sweetheart?" Michael smiles and asks.
"David is a very talented hockey player. Joseph is strong and smart in mechanics but what about Kevin he's just a little innocent kid? What about mom, how would she cope?"
Michael looks at his daughter and smiles and takes her hand and brushes her beautiful thick chestnut hair back over her shoulder and looks at her sweet angelic face."
"What about you?"
"What about me dad?"
"If something goes wrong today and God chooses to take me home today, what about you?"
"I'd do everything in my power to help mom finish raising Kevin and to take care of our farm."
"But what about you? How would you cope?" Sarah stands to her feet and looks at her dad.
"Dad there is only one way I'd know how to cope." Michael looks up at his daughter with a puzzled look. "I'll be right back," she says to her dad. She is gone about eighteen or nineteen seconds and returns with her Bible. She places it in her father's big strong hands. "Daddy this is how I'd cope." Michael smiles. "That's a great way to start!!" He hands Sarah's Bible back to her.
"Sarah open your Bible to I Peter 5:7." Sarah finds the verse. Read that to your dad:
Casting all your cares upon him; for he careth for you.
Michael gets up and smiles at Sarah. "Don't forget Sarah always cast all your cares on him and you will be just fine." Michael stands to his feet, grabs Sarah gently by each side of her face and kisses her on her forehead. "I love you my beautiful precious daughter!" Michael smiles and says as he walks back into his house. Sarah holds her Bible tight to her chest and goes down to

the last step that leads up to the porch that leads to their home. Sees the sun break through from behind a cloud, smiles and whispers "I Love you God!! Thanks for my dad."

Peter and Stephanie pull into the yard. Sarah goes into the house, grabs her dad's suitcase for him. Donna June, Michael, and Sarah all get in Pete and Stephanie's car. As they arrive at the hospital and register, Donna June escorts Michael to the surgery prep area. Donna June tries so hard to be strong. But her body gently trembles a bit, and a tear falls out of her eye. Micheal smiles and hugs her. "Don't you worry. Don't you worry. I'll be seeing you soon!" He wipes away her year. "I love you Michael."
"I love you to,"

At 5:24 pm, Pete looks at his watch. "Pete, what time is it?" asks Donna June.
"It's 5:24 pm Donna June. Sarah gets up out of her chair and looks out the window of the waiting room. After three or four minutes Sarah sits in her chair again. Then comes a smiling face that Donna June knows. Dr. McKinley says, "good afternoon everyone."
"Hello, Dr. McKinley," Donna June smiles and replies.
"I just wanna let you all know that surgery went wonderful. We finished up about twenty five to thirty minutes ago. Michael did wonderful."
All four beautiful souls in that room begin to smile. Well five souls including Dr. McKinley's but he was already smiling!
"You can see him after 7:30 pm tonight but he probably won't be very responsive to anyone until the morning."
"Dr. McKinley, thanks so much for everything!" replies Donna June.
"You're welcome. He will be on the fourth floor on the southwest wing."
"Ok, thank you."
"You're welcome. Bye bye," says Dr. McKinley.
"Wow, wonderful news," says Stephanie.
"I'll say," Sarah smiles and says.
"Donna June, do you know what Michael is facing for treatment ahead?" asks Pete.

"Not yet Pete." Donna June smiles and says.
"Excuse me everyone," says Donna June, "I'm gonna go call Kevin, David and Joseph and tell them the good news!"
"Sure," says Pete. As Donna June exits the room, Sarah smiles and says, "Pete and Stephanie thanks for everything you have done for our family and for mom and dad!"
"Oh, it's our pleasure," says Stephanie. "It's such a relief to know everything went well for dad!"
"I'm sure he may have a few challenging days ahead but always know and remember Sarah, Stephanie and I are just a phone call away.

Chapter 14: Hockey Night in Canada in St. Croix, NB

"Dad, dad, dad!"
"Yes Joseph, over here son. I'm just finishing up milking."
"Hurry dad, it's 7:29 pm we got thirty-one minutes to shower, get a snack, and turn on the TV. We don't wanna get behind and miss the first night off the official season."
Micaeal laughs and says, "Ya and the official theme song. Da, da, dat, da, da, da, da, dat, da, da!! Oh the good ole hockey night in Canada theme song!!!
"Hello, Hello."
"Hi, Pete in here!!"
"Hi guys better hurry as Pete looks at his watch! Thirty minutes to game time."
"We are Pete," Joseph smiles and says.
"Who's this little guy?" asks Joseph.
"Oh, that's my grandson Conner, he's five we got him for the weekend, hope it's okay?" asks Pete.
"Hi Connor, hi there!!" Michael smiles and says.
"Are you kidding?" says Joseph, the more the merrier!!! We're happy to have him."
Joseph is the last one out the barn man door and he shut off the lights. Michael, Connor and Pete all go into the house. Joseph is the last man in. Kevin looks up at his big brother. "Come on big brother twenty four minutes to game time," Kevin smiles and says.
"I'm coming buddy," replies Joseph. Sarah, Donna June, Stephanie are in the living room. Pete and Conner go in and sit down.
"Dad, take the shower first," shouts Joseph.

"Ok, son." Within six minutes Michael is showered and back down the stairs. As Joseph walks down the stairs,he goes into the kitchen, grabs two mixing bowls and sets them in the living room.
"Need help big bro?" asks Saraha
"No, I'm good. But thank you." He grabs eight glasses and a big picture of lemonade out of the fridge. And a big boy plain humpty dumpty potato chips.
"Everyone likes lemonade?"
"I love it," Connor says.
The Gallaghers and Pete and Stephaine giggle. Joseph pours the first glass and gives it to Connor! There you go buddy! Michael and Kevin open the chips and put them into the mixing bowls.
"7:53 pm turn on the TV," Michael asks Sarah. "Ok. dad."
She replies, "everyone take a seat." "Now we are joined by Mr. Larry Nicols head scout for the Maple Leafs. Larry had a lot of talk on the streets of Toronto. Apparently the Leafs got three new players right out of the box this season. "Yes, thanks Bob." "Can you tell me a little bit about them." "Yes, he played for a junior team we drafted out of Vancouver. He's a defense man. He's a great skater. Very quick, very powerful. Yes a lot of people were saying if the Leafs had a little better defense and goaltending they'd be unstoppable." "Well we're trying." Larry chuckles and laughs. "So I understand the second prospect is a goaltender." "Yes, he's a young guy from New Brunswick, shows a lot of great potential!" "Yes for sure, I believe we got a clip of him talking to reporters after the Chicago Toronto game." "Your second game in the NHL Stephen, you guys are on a roll, you had a three to one win at home with your first exhibition game with the Canadians. Pretty exciting."
"Look, look it's Stephen," Sarah points and smiles and says!
"Ya, I was pretty nervous my first game but I went out and did my best."
"Ya, and it was great, you played all three periods and did great. And tonight you and your team had a two to zero shutout victory here in Chicago over the Blackhawks."

"Yes, I'm really proud. These are exhibition games just for fun, but forty shots on goal in my second pre game ever. I hope I can keep this momentum going."
"Thanks, Stephen, best of luck to you."
"Thanks."
"Wow Larry, very, very impressive."
"Yes, thanks Bob, we are very proud of Stephen and his efforts. Yes and just like the song says a one to zero less on the third exhibition game against the Bruins but thirty two shots fired on goal just like the son says two outta three ain't bad!!!
"No, not bad at all."
"Three minutes to game time Larry, tell us very quickly about this third new player."
"He is from New Brunswick as well. We were debating umm whether or not to put him in center or not, but he told Mr. McNamara and myself ---
"Mom, mom, listen, listen," Sarah smiles and says.
"I am hunny."
"And he told his coaches ever since he was four or five he played right wing, that's what he is most comfortable with. So we're gonna leave him on the right wing."
"Yes the new defense man I believe his name is Todd Petten?"
"Yes, Todd Petten, Bob that's correct."
"In his first three NHL exhibition games total of twelve shots on goal for all three game and three assists credited to him and one goal. Pretty impressive for a big defenseman who hands back!
"Yep for sure Bob, his primary role is enforcer but hey we're the Leafs you know!! We're open to all players scoring goals!! Even the goalie if possible." Larry and Bob chuckles.
"And the last guy David Gallagher ummm four goals fired on net in his first game. No credit and no assist second game, six goals fired on net, one assist that game and his last game against the Bruins thirteen goals fired on net. Pretty impressive."
"Yep, we're happy with all three players."
"As well you should be," replies Bob.
"Ok Mr. Larry Nicols, thanks for taking the time to be with us."
"You're welcome Bob."

"Welcome everybody to the first game of the NHL season of regular play!! Detroit Red Wings go up against the Toronto Maple Leafs tonight at Maple Leaf Gardens. Welcome to Hockey night in Canada," as the USA national anthem is being played. As soon as the Canadian one begins, everybody stands in that living room in respect and when it is done, the gardens explode into cheering. "Ok here we go Detroit wins the face off go past the blueline a hard slap shot onto the net right out of the box, saved beautifully by Theriault. Theriault clears it out. Bradshaw and Petten start up. Petten is smashed into the boards. Petten is knocked down but gets up again quickly. Thomas fired one in quickly. Great save by Theriault. Ryscheck clears it to the blue line, two guns for Petten. Petten moves, keeps control of the puck Bentley takes Petten to the boards. Whistle blows that's the first penalty of the night to Petten for high sticking. Bob let's replay that real quick." "Sure Andrew." "Yes right there Bob. You see as Petten turns to shove on Bentley with his shoulder his stick was high. Here's the official ruling. Tom White referee,penalty charged to Maple Leafs two minutes to Petten high sticking." The crowd begins to boo. But that's hockey. "Ok, here we go Andrew. Thirty-one seconds remain in the penalty box for Petten. Detroit has been relentless on this power play in ninety second four shots on Theriault. Yes Theriault so far has managed to stop everyone. Nothing new under the sun for Detroit. They are a team noted to come hard and come fast." "Absolutely Andrew and especially on power plays."
"Man this is such a great game!!" Yells out Pete.
"I'll say," replies Joseph.
"Twenty seconds Toronto cleared it out to center but look Donaldson takes it away oh no around the one long Maple Leaf defenseman. Here's a shot of Theriault from about nine feet out of his helmet. It's in front of him he clears Donaldson and Smith tries to bat it in as Jones falls into Theriault. This is crazy three onto one, five seconds remain." Ref blows whistle. "Andrew this kid from New Brunswick is phenomenal but there's only so much he can do!!"
"Yes Bob but he needs Petten back for the help."

Miracle From First Pit Pond

"Well Andrew these three new prospects are paving their worth to the Leafs. Ok now everyone is up. Look, look at this. Jones takes a swing at Theriault but misses. Theriault drops the gloves three Leafs quickly get between Theriault and Jones now about four players are talking trash and one more Leaf player comes over to look at this Theriault is trying to come around. This is nuts!!! Let me tell you something Bob. New Brunswick is one of the smallest provinces in our Country but there's nothing small about the heart of this kid!!
"Whoa hoa go Stephen,'' shouts little Kevin!!!
Joseph, Pete, Stephanie, Michael, Donna June, Connor all laugh.
"Listen Andrew the fans are on their feet!! As loud as World War II all chanting Theriault, Theriault, Theriault. Stephen gives a big wave to the hometown crowd!! If this is any indication of what's to come, we got an exciting, exciting year of hockey ahead of us!!"

"Ok, here we go again. Detroit wins face off with two seconds left in power play Toronto coach calls for a change up and roars Petten out of the penalty box Detroit slaps one in just wide of Theriault's net! Gallagher is now on the ice Petten starts up the side. Passed to Johnson, Johnson goes around Donaldson two Leafs against one Redwing. Johnson passes to Gallagher, "Go David, go Daivd," shouts Michael. Gallagher looks back and raises his stick ready to fire. Knocks puck back to Petten seven feet behind with his left skate. Petten shoots he scores!!! Oh, man what a sweet bit of work by Petten and Gallagher!!! Four minutes and forty-one seconds into the first period Leafs lead one nothing!! With a goal being credited to Todd Peten and an assist to David Gallagher!!!"

"Ok back at center ice, the Leafs win the face off and so on and so on until there is nineteen minutes and thirty-two seconds on the clock! Donaldson now tries to poke on past Theriault. Theriault cleared Gillmore. Gillmore passes to Petten. Petten goes by the centerline Petten fires it into the left side. It bounces off the backboards. Jones tries to clear it out but he's overtaken by Gallagher. Gallagher comes around the side he tries to poke it in. David Gallagher off the pad of Benoir. Jones clears it passed the blue line. Eleven seconds remain. Gillmore passes to Cote. Petten

is coming up past the center! Seven seconds over to Petten. Peten passes to Gilmore. Gilmore fires at four seconds! Gallagher takes the puck passes to Cote. Cote shoots, he scores!!! One second remaining on the clock. Daniel Cote!!! Being credited a goal and another assist to David Gallagher. Red wings win face off and that's it Bob. Toronto leads two to zero after the first period."
"Wow, what a great game," Sarah says!!
"What did you think of old scrappy Steve, Sarah?" asks Joseph.
"Ha, ha, ha he is a little scrappy tonight!!"
"It's kinda funny cause Stephen is so sweet and polite!!"
"Yep, but you ain't gonna mess with his net," says Donna June. The phone rings, Joseph says, "I got it."
"Hello! Oh hi LeRoy how are ya?"
"Oh, we're great!!"
"Oh ya, we are watching it!!"
"You're watching it with your dad, that's great!! When did he get home?"
"Yesterday around noon."
"Where was he this trip?"
"Laredo, Texas."
"Well I'm glad he's home! LeRoy's dad was a long haul truck driver. What's that? Your dad called him scrappy Stephen."
"That's funny cause that's what I called him to Sarah! What? I know it's awesome!!! Ok LeRoy have a good night!! See ya at church tomorrow!! Bye bye. Ha, ha, ha" Joseph chuckles. You Guys wanna hear something funny? LeRoy's dad referred to Stephen as scrappy Steve too!!!"
"Ha, ha, ha that's funny." they all laugh and say.
"Ok now back with Andrew and Bob and Don Cherry, with coaches corner. Well Don says Andrew what did you think of that?"
"Pretty exciting first period wouldn't you say?"
"Listen," says Don Cherry. "Hockey is alive and well in the world!!! It's alive and well here in Toronto tonight. What did you think of the first period?" asks Bob.

Miracle From First Pit Pond

"As I said hockey is alive and well and apparently it's alive and well on the frozen ponds of New Brunswick where scrappy Steve and Gallagher hail from!!!"

The Gallagher house erupts in laughter in unison. Sarah says, "this scrappy Steve thing is catching on like wildfire!"

Andrew says, " yes great goaltending by Stephen Theriault."

"Yes," replies Cherry, "and this big new brute from Vancouver Petten. He's got size, he's got bite! And I absolutely love the way Gallagher sets Petten up for goals. Yes all players, Gallagher, Theriault, and Petten seem to be well versed together. Well we know Gallagher and Theriault played together on frozen ponds in NewBrunswick.

"Let me tell ya something," replies Don Cherry. "With the verteran talent the Leafs possess and have, players like Douggie Gilmore and Anderson with this new dream team, Larry Nicols has put together, Petten, Gallagher and Theriault, I'm telling you right now, the Leafs will be a force to be reckoned with."

"Absolutely." says Andrew. "Don, I wanted to ask you," says Bob. "Gallagher and Theriault coming off the ponds of New Brunswick into the pro's of NHL. Do you have any comments on that? What's your feelings on that?"

"My feelings are," replies Don Cherry. "A wise man once said, the greatest of journeys begin with a single step. These boys might have come from the ponds of NB but Bobby Hull and Rocket Richard started on ponds and they greatly contributed to the NHL.

"Don thank you very much," replies Andrew. Period two coming right up.

"And now back to Maple Leaf Gardens. As period two begins, the action is hard and fast. Stephen endures eight shots in second period not one slip by. Benoir, Detroit's goalie endures five shots but none get by.

Little Connor almost made it through the whole second period, but sleep over takes him. Sarah takes him upstairs and gently lays him on her bed and covers him with a blanket. As Sarah returns back down stairs, Joseph asks, "any more lemonade, anyone?"

"I'll have more please," says Donna June. "Half a glass for me," says Pete.

"You got it." Joseph smiles and says.
"Great game," says Stephanie, "Toronto's holding their own with the two nothing lead!!"
Sarah returns back downstairs and smiles and says, "ya thanks to the efforts of scrappy Steve."
They all smile and laugh.
"So Micheal are ya starting to dig and bring in potatoes on Monday?"
"Yep, 7:15 am has been nice sunny weather since last Wednesday and the long range says tomorrow and Monday and Tuesday are sunny as well. Time to get 'em up and get 'em in!! There's a twenty pound bag in it for ya if you wanna come help, Pete," replies Michael.
"Oh, I'll come help, but you don't have to give me a twenty pound bag."
"Are you kidding?" asks Micaeal. "You and Stephanie have been nothing but kind to us during my whole cancer ordeal and if memory serves me right, you're taking me to my last cancer treatment Thursday at 9:00 am. What about you and the family?"
"When Stephanie and I accidentally backed the half ton into the ditch three winters ago. David, Joseph and Sarah couldn't get up there quick enough to tow us out. And anything from a chain to a big pipe wrench you folks always loan us your stuff."
"Well I'd say we are both extremely lucky to have great friends and neighbours in one another!!!" replies Stephanie.
"Amen Stephanie," Donna June smiles and says.

"Ok, here we go in the third period. The Detroit coach is pointing down to Petten. Let me tell ya Andrew this kid is definitely earning his paycheque tonight. Absolutely Bob and maybe their feelings are for Detroit, you take out the Alpha wolf and the rest will scatter. We will see Bob. Detroit wins the face off down through the center comes Jones and O'Brien. Petten skates backwards. O'Brien passes to Jones, Petten goes for the grab. He misses a wrist shot in from Jones. Theriault deflects away. Cleared out by Anderson, Gallagher and Gillmore fly up. Oh Gallagher is checked hard to the boards by Thomas. Gallagher is slow to get up. Detroit

Miracle From First Pit Pond

back down the ice Thomas takes a shot goes wide. Petten tries to clear it out and it's blocked by O'brien. O'brien fires and goes wide. Here comes Gallagher and Anderson down to help out. Thomas slams Gallagher to the boards again. Gallagher clears it up to center. Mikechoff starts down for Detroit slaps one in from the blue line. Just goes wide of Theriault. Andrew the Red Wings are really putting the pressure on. Thomas checks Petten but Gallagher clears it past center. O'Brien slams it back down, Thomas checks Petten again and elbows Petten but no call is made. Finally a whistle for icing. Thomas is apointing at Petten. Petten gets to his feet, motions the elbow toward the ref, he throws up his hands. I guess he didn't see it. Oh look look, Thomas is laughing and calling out Gallagher. Gallagher is pushed by O'Brien. Gallagher goes around to Thomas. Thomas drops the gloves. Gallagher drops the gloves. Here we go, here we go. Oh Gallagher endures two big right hands to his nose.

"Get that bully big brother." Sarah jumps up and shouts to the TV. "Gallaghers got Thomas by the bottom of his shirt oh a third right hand. By Thomas right into Gallagher's nose. A lot of blood is flowing from Gallagher. Gallagher gets Thomas' shirt up over his head. Thomas can't see oh they're fighting Irsish now. Gallagher is just pummelling Thomas in the ears and jaws with rights, the crowd erupts. Thomas is down to one knee. Now all the referees and linesmen are trying to pull Gallagher off of him. Petten comes up to Gallagher and pats him on his back!! Thomas looks dazed and confused to say the least! This reminds me of the Gretezsky, Oleander fight in 1983. Yes Andrew but Gretezsky got the Oilers the Cup. Well I tell ya what Bob. The heart and drive these three new prospects got the cup could be making its way to Toronto. Amen to that and I think we both agree you're gonna show all these new guys respect for sure or your gonna be taught it! Ha ha ha replies Bob. Yes for sure, you're gonna give the respect or scrappy Steve and the fighting Irish Gallagher will give it to ya in a way you won't like. Toronto coach Milbury is shaking his head.

"Yay David!!" Donna June shakes her head as Sarah and Joseph high five each other.

"Ha, ha ,ha what did you think of that Michael?"

"That big bad brute got taught some manners by David ay?"

"That's my boy," Micaeal smiles and says!

"Ok, looks like the referees have made their decisions. Here we go Bob," says Andrew.

"For Toronto number thirty-four David Gallagher two minutes for fighting. The crowd boos. For Detroit, number fifteen Clyde Thomas two minutes for fighting. The crowd boos. Oh wait, wait Thomas goes into the penalty box smiling. Wait Andrew I think there's more. For Detroit team, Clyde Thomas, three minutes unsportsmanlike conduct. The home crowd erupts in cheering. Petten goes down to Stephen Theriault. They raise their sticks up high and wave to the crowd. Oh Andrew look at this Thomas is punching the penalty box glass. He does not like that call. "Well perhaps it will teach him to use more manners," replies Andrew. Look at this LaFrate and Gillmore and Anderson and all the Leafs are going up to Gallagher and giving him a high five. Man what a night of NHL action in Toronto. Ok finally all players take their positions 17:53 remaining in this third and final period. Here we go Toronto wins the face off. The game goes on and on till there are two minutes remaining. Andrew what's our thoughts on the final two here, asks Bob. Hopefully the Leafs have their win here but Detroit has hammered them hard all night long. Fifty-two shots on goal. Young Stephen Theriault has been great but the Leafs have only retaliated with thirty two shots on goal. But they were able to get two of the thirty-two past Benoir. Here we go, Leafs win the face off, LaFrate passes to Anderson. Anderson starts up. Checked by O'Brien into the boards. Jones takes control passes to Mikeoff. Mikeoff fires from the blueline great stick save by Theriault. Anderson fires it up. Gillmore and Petley Gillmore fired wide. Here comes big bad Clyde Thomas back down the ice one minute twenty seconds remaining. Thomas is checked by Gallagher into the boards. Petten takes control of the puck. He fires one in great save by Benoir. One minute to go. Jones skates down the ice hard and fast, He passes to Thomas. Thomas fires one in front of the center; it goes off the pad of Theriault. Donaldson tries to poke it in from the side. Theriault knocks it off to the right. LaFrate passes to Petten. Petten darts up, he fires one and bounces off the stick of Benoir. Gillmore wrist shots the rebound. It bounces to the left.

Miracle From First Pit Pond

Thirty-three seconds remaining. Hydelchuck gets it to the blue line. Gallagher is there. Gallagher slap shots. Ohh David Gallagher shoots and he scores!! Twenty-eight seconds remaining what a great goal by David Gallagher.

Every Gallagher and Stephanie and Pete all stand to their feet. The applause from that living room in St. Croix, New Brunswick was strong and loud enough to wake a salmon sleeping in the St. Croix river!!

"Oh, how sweet it is," replies Andrew. "Twenty-eight seconds remaining. Leafs up three to nothing on Detroit. David is smiling ear to ear! With a bruised swollen nose and all after David can break free of his teammates he skates down to Stephen. They hug one another!! Then all of a sudden the other Leafs join in for a group hug. The players on the Leafs bench all applaud. The Gardens erupts with sudden applause and cheering!! Oh how sweet it is, says Andrew to Bob. David Michal Gallagher's first NHL goal of the season amongst his fans and his teammates at Mapleleaf Gardens! "How sweet it is indeed Andrew," replies Bob!! Twenty-seven second remaining Toronto wins the face off. Jones and Thomas start down. Jones fires it and it goes wide. Petten clears to the centerline Mikeoff fires it back to the blueline. Twelve seconds remain Petten passes to Gillmore. Gillmore is knocked to the boards by Jones. Ten seconds remaining. Mike fires it down and Petten intercepts Petten to Anderson. Anderson fires it and is interrupted by Thomas. Thomas start down. Thomas is checked by Petten. Jones picks up the puck four seconds remaining. Mikeoff shoots it goes wide two seconds later Petten has the puc regeuler season at home in the Gardens. Coming up Shawn Anderson in conversation with Andrew and Bob. Back in two minutes after this commercial break.
"Wow, pretty proud of those guys," replies Michael.
"What a great game!" replies Pete.
"Oh, we're back with Shawn Anderson, center for the Toronto Maple Leafs. Shawn a great effort tonight by all! And congratulations on your victory!!!"
"Thanks Andrew!"

"Wow, some very fast paced hockey tonight!"
"Yes, for sure, we were hopping right to it!"
"Detroit is a team known for fast hard hitting hockey."
"Oh, for sure."
"But in summer training camp we knew with teams like Philly and Detroit we gotta take it right back to them."
"And what do you think about the three new members to the team this year?"
"I feel all young, all strong. But I gotta tell ya Stephen Theriault is just whaling on it coming right out of the box!! A shut out tonight and a shutout in one of the exhibition games!"
"It's phenomenal!"
"It's great!"
"Shawn thanks for talking with us tonight!!!"
"Great action tonight Bob."
"Yes, I'm glad to see the Leafs coming out with a great mix of the old and new. Andrew we're just getting word that Todd Petten, Stephen Teriault, and David Galagher are on their way to talk to us two minute commercial break and we will be back live from Toronto this is Hockey night in Canada.
"Guys, thanks so much for coming Todd Petten, David Gallagher and scrappy Steve Theriault!!!"
"Thanks for having us Andrew," replies Todd.
"Stephen, let's start with you. A shutout in one of the exhibition games and a shutout tonight after being pummeled all night long. Pretty impressive stuff."
"Thanks, but I trained hard and I owe so much of this to my teammate and best friend David Gallagher. He worked with me a lot back home and he saw potential in me I didn't know I had."
"Bob, we've seen this in a lot of players haven't we! Another player can mentor and help immensely."
"Oh, for sure and sometimes once a talent is tapped into the possibilities are endless!!"
"Thanks Bob," replies Stephen.
"Now what would you say is one of the things he told you to help the most?"

"Well, Bob I can't let the cat out of the bag fully here ya know!" says Stephen. "Gotta keep some things secret, ya know!"
"Easy, easy there scrappy Steve." Bob laughs and says, "what happened there tonight Steve?" asks Andrew.
"The jersey said Maple Leafs and the back says twelve Theriault. But for a minute there we thought it was Billy Smith from the Islanders."
"Ha, ha, ha," Stephen laughs. "Well when he got in my crease, he fell in not me to him but then to give me attitude. And wanna get physical well you know maybe time for a little whoopin ya know? That's my crease. I'm gonna protect it!"
"This is awesome," says Andrew. "You don't mess with scrappy Steve Theriault!!!"
"Todd congrats on your win tonight!"
"Thanks, Bob."
"What do ya think of your new teammates here?"
"Bob, I gotta tell ya they're just great."
"Yes, watching you guys tonight you and David seem to have a great chemistry together."
"Thanks, Bob. I've played hockey for over eleven years but David has a year or two up on me and there is always something to learn!!!"
"Todd congrats on your win tonight."
"Thanks Andrew."
"How do you feel on the ice alongside David."
"David reminds me a lot of Bobby Orr in his style of playing."
"He is looking awesome."
"Thanks, Todd."
And last but not least David Micaeal Gallagher.
"Hi, Bob."
"How's the nose by the way?"
"Ha, ha, ha a little sore but I'll be alright."
"Thomas of course a big tough guy, an enforcer but you took him to school."
"Bob where Stephen and I come from there's a lot of great people but once in a while we have run into a bad one. Well where we come from it's called taking them to the woodshed."
"Well you took Thomas there alright," replies Andrew.

"David, congrats on the win tonight!" Thanks Andrew.
"Boys I gotta tell ya big night for you! Your first NHL penalty, first NHL goal! One goal and two assists for the night is not bad, not a bad debut into the NHL at all."
"Thank you!"
"The Leafs have been my team since I was a little kid. You know I'm just so happy to be here!!! It's an honour to play for the leafs and to have great teammates like LaFrate and Anderson, Todd and scrappy Steve here!!!"
Everyone laughs.

"David, Don Cherry on coach's corner tonight referred to you and Todd and Stephen as the Leafs new dream team. What do you think of that?"
"Well anytime Don Cherry says something good about ya's you know it's a great badge of honour!!"
"Thanks David, Thanks guys."
"You're welcome," Todd and David and Stephen all say.
"Final thoughts coming in a moment from Bob and I. Your watching hockey night in Canada on CBC."

"Wow, that was great!!" Michael smiles and says.
"Yes sir, I'm glad they had a win for their first official game."
"I'll go warm the car up for Conner, Stephanie."
"Ok, sweetheart," replies Stephanie.
Michael walks to the kitchen with Pete.
"Well I'll see ya shortly after 7:00 am on Monday Pete! Thanks so much for all the help."
"It's my pleasure!!!"
"Thanks for the twenty pounds of spuds!! But you don't have to do that!!"
"It's my pleasure, buddy!"
"Pete starts up the car. Sarah goes upstairs, gently picks up Connor off of her bed and lays him in Stephanie's arms.
"Thanks for a great evening," Stephanie says.
"You're welcome Stephanie," replies Donna June.

"Stephanie, your niece Heather VCR recorded the game tonight right?"

"Yes, before we came down, she called and said she was gonna do it."

"Wonderful! My friend Beth did too. Just thought I had two people do it, it would be a good thing to give David. His first NHL regular season game."

"Yes, and having two people do it, it's a good safety factor, if one tape broke or was defective or something, it's a good fail safe."

"For sure," Donna June smiles and says.

"And if they both come out good, I'll keep one for myself!"

"Great idea Donna June."

"Goodnight everyone!!"

"Goodnight," Sarah and Donna June and Joseph say. Kevin went up to his room and went to bed.

"Well we better get to bed. Eggs to gather, cows to milk, , then church!!"

"Dad?"

"Yes, Joseph?"

"You sleep in tomorrow I'll get up at 4:00 am to milk."

"Are you sure son?" asks Michael..

"I am dad yep!"

"Don't worry about the eggs," says Sarah.Kevin and I will get up at 8:00am to collect them then we will make breakfast!!"

"Well thank you my wonderful children!!"

"You're welcome, wonderful father." Sarah smiles and says. Donna June, Michael, Sarah and Joseph all share a laugh. In October of 1989 life was good on the Gallagher farm. But there's potatoes to get up and in one more cancer treatment to take. And a mortgage to pay through the long winter months. But the Gallaghers had love, the Gallaghers had faith. the Gallaghers had God and the Gallaghers had each other!! Life just may be ok.

Frederick Demerchant

Miracle From First Pit Pond

Chapter 15: Time for the Spring Playoffs

Well with the effort of all the Leafs, they made the playoffs!! David was excited as a pig is to see a slop hole!! David and his team had made it all the way to the Eastern Conference Championships who had won between Toronto Maple Leafs and the New York Rangers played for the cup.

Vancouver was waiting to play the winner. They won the series in five games over the Los Angeles Kings. But Buffalo had dragged out their series to a three to three series tie with their victory at home in Buffalo with a three to two win in overtime. Tonight was the big night May 10th in Toronto.
"Welcome to CBC Hockey Night in Canada game number seven of the Eastern Conference playoff series. I'm Bob Thompson with me as always Andrew Sullivan. "Andrew Hi!"
"Bob, good evening the streets are alive with electricity tonight in Toronto."
"Ohh man, can you ever feel it Andrew!! It's been just a phenomenal year, wonderful wonderful year for the Leafs. I mean where do you begin. Dougie Gilmore leading the team for goals. Al LaFrate is just like a wolf on defense. Andrew what about the wonderwork of Larry Nicols? I'm talking about what has proven to be what Don Cherry called them. The dream team!!! Todd Petten, David Gallagher and scrappy Stephen Theriault. These guys have just had a phenomenal first year in the pros Andrew all of them!!"
"Yes Todd Petten is a great enforcer fast, gritty and powerful. Twenty-five assists, twenty one goals in regular season play is not bad for a 6'2" 223 lbs defenceman. Scrappy Stephen Theriault. He was starting goalie in thirty seven of the forty four regular season games. Five shutout wins in regular season play 1504 shots on goal

only 101 goals got by him. For a non vetern goalie to have that kinda saving ratio. I mean what else do you say? It's just truly, truly amazing."

"Absolutely and young David Gallagher. David played in all forty four games in the regular season and scored twenty-seven goals and had seventy assists."

"Bob, that's one thing I love about young David Gallagher. I haven't seen the Leafs look this good in years! He sets up the other players! So quick and so well. I mean it's just magical to watch. Well let's hope David Gallagher and the rest of the Leafs will bring magic to the Gardens tonight. Three minutes to National anthem time. Game number seven Eastern Conference final. Bob Thompson, Andrew Sullivan we will be right back. CBC Hockey Night in Canada."

"Dad the game is about to start!!!"

"Thanks Sarah Elizabeth," Michael smiles and says as he kisses her on the cheek.

"Is mom and Kevin and Joseph watching tonight?"

"Kevin says he's gonna listen to this one up in his room on his radio. Mom is at a ladies meeting with the church. And Joseph left at 6:30 pm on his motorcycle but said he's gonna watch the game with Tanya at Tanya's house."

"Ok, hey are they official boyfriend and girlfriend now?"

"I don't think just yet sweetheart, but it's kinda looking that way!!"

"She's a nice girl."

"Yep and her family are nice people as well!!"

"I love ya dad. Gonna get some banana bread and ice tea for us to snack on."

"Ok, thanks sweetheart!!!!"

Meanwhile in a locker room in Toronto.

"So scrappy Stephen are you nervous tonight?" asks Todd.

"No, you think I would be, but I'm not."

"How about you, Todd?"

"Just a little."

"David how about you?" asks Todd.

"I'm a little nervous before every game. But I'm just gonna do my best!"

"One minute to game time," shouts the coach. The greatest thing wasn't how far the boys came this season, but that another soul was won for the kingdom of God. Stephen's and David's witness caused Todd to give his heart to Christ March 2, 1989 in Philadelphia, Pennsylvania.

"Better pray," says scrappy Steve.

"Who's doing the honours tonight?"

"I will." Todd smiles and says. The boys join hands "Dear Lord Jesus, Thank you for all the blessings you have given us! Tonight we ask for you to guide us and be with us on the ice. Thank you Lord for how far you have brought us this season!! Thanks for your love and my wonderful friends David and Stephen. In Jesus name, Amen." The boys go out. The USA anthem is played then the Canadian one. The Gardens erupt in cheering!! One minute left in the first period Buffalo one Toronto one. Here comes Anderson and Petten on a breakaway Anderson to Petten. Petten back to Anderson he shoots. Great save by Nicolson. Twenty-eight seconds left in the first period the Leafs battle to the closing bell it's tied up at one to one. Coach's corner coming up with Don Cherry. Buffalo one Toronto one tied up in the first period of the Eastern Conference Final. You're watching Hockey Night in Canada on CBC.

"What do you think dad? Do you think the Leafs can pull it off?" asks Sarah..

"Well sweetheart, statistically Buffalo had a better year, but hey it's the play off hockey!! Anything's possible."

Don gives his comments and the second and third periods are now gone. Well most of the third one there is three minutes left. It's tied two to two.

"Ok here we go Andrew Buffalo on a powerplay Anderson is in the penalty box for forty one more seconds for high sticking. Buffalo wins the face off. Johnson to Donaldson up comes Petten, Donaldson goes around he passes to Hadley, Hadley back to Johnson. Gallagher clears it to center. Picked up by Hextall. Hextall passes to Johnson slap shot in great save by Theriault. Eighteen seconds remaining in the penalty. Gallagher chasing

Donaldson. Donaldson fires Petten takes Donaldson to the boards wrist shot by Hextal off the pad of Theriault Johnson flicks it high off the arm of Theriault. Bounces to the side Petten trying to come around Hextell shoots he scores. Phillip Hextall has put Buffalo in the lead. Oh man Andrew what more could the Leafs have done? Absolutely Bob. Anderson with four seconds remaining in the penalty box. Patten and Gallagher work well together but one would take on to the boards another came crashing upon them. I don't know Bob, the Leafs are trying so hard, I'm not sure what else they can do.

Ok here we go two minutes and twenty-three seconds remaining the leafs battle right to the very end but they don't pull it off. Buffalo will face Vancouver in Vancouver in three days for game number one of the Stanley Cup Final. The Leafs form a line and Buffalo shakes their hands. David enjoys a laugh and a pat on the shoulder by Buffalo's Matt Dennelson.

Great game dad and a great season for Stephen and David huh?"
"Oh for sure. The power play goal was just too much to come back from in such a short period of time. He should feel very, very proud though Dad!"
"I'm going to bed now dad. Goodnight, I love you!!" Sarah gives her dad a great big hug and a kiss on the cheek."
"I love you sweetheart, goodnight."

The telephone rings. "Hello." replies Michael.
"Yes operator I'll accept a collect call from David."
"Hi dad how are ya!!!"
"I'm great, son! We just got done watching your big game!!"
"We tried so hard dad but we just couldn't pull it off tonight."
"Yes son power plays against you in the third period is never ever a good thing."
"I just called to tell you three things dad. First thing, thanks for all you and mom taught me!!! Can't believe I'm here playing for the Leafs. I never would have gotten here, had it not been for you and mom! The second thing is I love you very much, and the third thing is, I got a few loose ends to tie up here in Toronto and Todd, Stephen and I have things we gotta do next Saturday. It's a nice

new program the Leafs started called Rookies for Radicalness. We spend an afternoon with less fortunate kids and just talk with them and play hockey at the Gardens with them, then Subway caters lunch for us here at the Gardens. It's a good new program where we all try to make a difference. And I'm very, very proud to be a part of that."
"As well you should be son!!"
"That all sounds great!"
"But when that's done, I'll be home soon after!"
"That's great son, we can't wait to see you!"
"Ok, dad I love you very much. I'll see you soon. Say hi to everybody for me!"
"I will and you say hi to scrappy Stephen Theriault from us!"
"Ha, ha, ha, ha I will bye bye."

Micaeal looks at the TV and sits down for a minute. Andrew Sulllivan back with Bob Thompson being joined by scrappy Stephen Theriault and Al LaFrate. Guys thanks for joining us tonight.
"It's our pleasure, thanks for having us.""Al let's start with you. You guys battled so hard tonight but four power plays over you and two of them in the third period. When you're tied up, that's always a hard row to hoe isn't it?"
"Absolutely, Andrew. Every single man is crucial and you know a good thing but with the speed of Buffalo and a man advantage against you, it's hard it's definitely hard. I also think to that in the playoffs especially their gunning so hard against you anyway around ya that they can get."
"Scrappy Steve here did excellent but you know gotta try and keep it out past the blue lines at least. Al in your opinion being the vetern defenseman you are, is there more of a strategy or maybe a strategic way or a strategic approach for power plays?"
"Well Bob for power plays or not you gotta hand back you know to a degree but that extra man you know it's almost like their the cat and your the ball of yarn."
"Al thank you very much. Scrapy Stephen Theriault had a phenomenal year for you in your rookie season. In the playoffs alone you had two shutout games and the series with the Habs you

had in one game I think seventy-nine shots on goal. Ha, ha, ha, and you stopped them all but one. Pretty darned impressive."
"Yeah it keeps me pretty limber that's for sure."
"Yes I remember that night and that game. Seventy-nine shots on me but it's the playoffs you know it's like Al said they're coming at you hard and fast."
"Stephen apparently you have set an NHL record in your rookies season with most power play goals stopped by a goalie. In the regular season."
"Oh, thanks Andrew, I wasn't aware. My philosophy is quite simple really I just try to protect that net. You know I've learned so much from Al and veteran players. But like I said before. David Gallagher has taught me the most."
"Yes when you guys were playing pond hockey back home in NB apparently David pulled double duty as a coach."
"Well David has such a love, respect and passion, a pure beautiful passion for the game, he taught me so much. And I'm very grateful to the Leafs and very grateful to Mr. Gerry McNamara, and Mr. Larry Nicols and the veterans like Al and Anderson and Douggie Gillmore for all they have helped me with and coached me with! I'm just so honoured and proud to be here!"
"We're honoured and proud to have you!"
"Thanks Andrew, thanks Bob." "The Eastern Conference final three to two for Buffalo. From Toronto I'm Andrew Sullivan with Bob Thompson, Al LaFrate and scrappy Stephen Theriault saying goodnight for Hockey Night in Canada on CBC."
Michael shuts off his TV and goes to bed. The next morning it's just an absolutely beautiful early spring day in New, Brunswick, Canada.
Honey,, honey are you in here," Donna June says in the beautiful early dawn's light.
"just down stairs making a coffee.
 Michael smiles and says!"
"Hi, cutie pie!" Donna June smiles and says.
"Well, hey good lookin'," Michael smiles and replies.
"I brought you a coffee!"
"Well thank you very much.

Miracle From First Pit Pond

"yes out milking and gathering eggs," replies Donna June.
"You know Donna June, I'm so proud of them. When I was sick they all chipped in extra hard."
"The Lord blessed us with great kids," Donna June smiles and says.
"He sure did!"
"As the days got longer and longer one late May morning around May 23rd to be exact, Joseph and his dad got up one morning at 4:05 am to start the milking, but they noticed the lights were on in the barn.
"Dad you were the last person in the barn last night weren't you?"
"Yes, son I was."
"Did you forget to shut the lights off?"
"No, I'm positive I shut them off."
As Joseph and his dad get closer to the barn they hear 88.5 Fm out of Bangor Maine gospel music in the early morning hours. And the man door was left open three or four inches.
"Hello, hello," Joseph says as he goes into the door.
"Good morning big brother!" Joseph and his dad can't believe what they see!! David is sitting on the little milking stool milking away. They both run to him. He gets up and smiles and hugs each one of them!!
"David, David, welcome home son!!"
"Welcome home!!" Joseph is laughing.
"Two questions, first one, how did you get here?"
"I had a rental waiting for me at the airport."
"Well where is it?"
"We didn't see it in the yard?"
"I just parked it up the road in the turnoff at the edge of our property."
"I caught the last flight into Fredericton. I landed at 11:35 pm, got a Big Mac at Prospect Street McDonalds then I just crashed at McAdam in the car for a few hours and I just drove out and started milking."
"How come you parked up the road, son?"
"I just wanted to surprise ya's."
"And what a great surprise!!!" Michael smiles and says.
"When do you gotta have the car back?" asks Joseph.

"Is that your second question?" asks David. Joseph pulls the brim of David's hat down over his forehead. "No." replies Joseph.
"I gotta have it back by 5:00 pm, I was hoping you could borrow dad's car and pick me up."
"Sure, no problem!"
"Great." David smiles and says! "Then we can go to Prospect Street McDonalds after and you can buy me another Big Mac."
Joseph giggles, "hey why don't you buy me one Mr. NHLer?"
Michael, David and Joseph all share a laugh!
"Jeez little brother it's so great to have you home!!"
"Amen to that!!" replies Michael.
"My second question is how long are you home for?"
"I'm home till August 7th gotta flyout at 12:00pm and training camp starts on the 8th at 8:00 am."
"Well, welcome home son!!"
"Do you and Joseph got the milking ok?"
"Sure dad, no problem." replies Joseph.
"Well, I'll go in and start breakfast."
"Thanks, dad," replies David.

As David and Joseph finish up the milking, Michael prepares bacon, eggs, red river cereal, raisin bread toast and homemade biscuits. Sarah is the first one downstairs.
"Good morning dad."
"Good morning sweetheart."
"Gee dad quite a bit for a Thursday morning isn't it?"
"You're a growing girl Sarah you gotta eat!!" Sarah gives her dad a hug and a kiss on the cheek. Kevin comes downstairs.
"Good morning buddy."
"Hi dad!"
"Hope you're hungry buddy."
All of a sudden the door is open with laughter from two brothers.
"Oh my goodness, David." Sarah runs over and hugs her brother!
"Oh my goodness David when did you get here?"
"About two and a half hours ago sis!"
"David, hi, hi,hi," Kevin shouts and runs and jumps into his brother David's arms.

"Hey buddy, my how you've grown!!!" I was figuring I'd come home and say in shape by working on the farm all summer, but I think all I gotta do is carry you around."
Sarah gets six plates down from the cupboard for her dad, and he starts dishing out all the great food.
"David Michael Gallagher, is that you?" a friendly voice says from upstairs!
"It sure is mom!!!" Donna June runs down quickly.
"Welcome home son!!!"
"Aww thanks mom, it's great to be home!"
They all sit at the table and hold hands.
"Sarah Elizabeth, will you do the honours please?" asks her dad.
"Sure dad. Dear Jesus thanks for all your blessings, thanks for bringing David safely home to us. And thanks for this great breakfast! Bless dad's hands that prepared it! In Jesus name Amen.
The family has a great breakfast and same great laughs. David looks at each member of his family and thinks to himself how greatly blessed he is!

Frederick Demerchant

Chapter 16: The Leafs are on Fire

"Scrappy Steve you are hot tonight buddy!!" "Thanks Todd."
"Last game of the regular season and this year we are ranked number one in our division."
"Todd never count your chickens before they hatch," says McGuire.
"I'm not counting them but I hope I get the chance to hoist that cup in a couple months."
"We all do buddy!" replies Shawn Anderson.
"Great way to end the season. Theriault another shutout! Thanks Clark." Stephen smiles and says.
"You can learn a lot in a professional sports locker room David thinks to himself. "Guys hey guys," says Stephen. I want ya's all to know not one of these shutouts would be possible without all your guy's hard work! Most of the guys all smile and say, "Thanks Stephen."
David goes over to his friend, he nudges him from behind, his shoulder to Stephen's shoulder.
"Scrappy, how's it going?"
"Ha, ha, ha," Stephen chuckles.
"Not too, too bad. It's 4:43 pm. How about we go down to Mike's cafe and have supper on me?" asks David.
"I'll go on one condition," replies Stephen.
"What's your condition pal?" asks David.
"Supper is on me!!" Stephen smiles and says.
"You, drive a hard bargain," David smiles and says!"

As the boys have a shower and change the traffic isn't to, too bad this Saturday evening so the boys make it to Mike's cafe in twenty four minutes or so. As they go in and take a seat at a table, they see a familiar face.

"Hi guys!! So nice to see ya's!!!"

"Well hi Tamara," Stephen smiles and says.

"Hi Tamara, how's it going?" asks David.

"Just great," Tamara smiles and says congratulations on your great season!!"

"Hey, thanks a lot Tamara!" Stephen smiles and says, "no problem there scrappy."

Stephen giggles and David does as well. You know what I think Stephen?" Asks Tamara.

"I think they got you all wrong?"

"What do you mean Tamara?" asks Stephen.

"Well you're a nice polite Maritime young man, they should call you sweetie pie Steve."

"Aww thanks Tamara, that's very kind of you."

"Careful, Tamara." David smiles and says his head will swell up and you won't get him through the door. They all chuckle and Stephen gently punches David's shoulder.

"Whoa, whoa, easy there, scrappy!! Tamara smiles and says. They all share a chuckle again.

"Well guys, I better get back to my friends and my lemon maringine pie. Try some for dessert guys. It's awesome." "We will," says David. "Is it as good as the warm toasted ham and cheese?"

"Oh, that's a tough one," Tamara says.

"Both excellent," Tamara smiles and says!

"Have a great evening," guys you to Tamara! Stephen and David reply.

A friendly approaching waitress, says "hi guys would you like menus today?"

"Sure," replies Stephen.

"Can I start ya's off with a drink?"

"I'll have a large white milk," Stephen smiles and says.

"Me too please," says David.

"So are you nervous going into the playoffs?" asks David.

"Just a little," replies Stephen.

"How about you?"
"No I'm not nervous," says David, I'm just gonna do my best!
The waitress brings their milk.
"All set to order guys?"
"Yes, I'll have the BLT platter and can I have a side of gravy too, please?"
"Sure," she smiles and says.
"And for you?" she asks David.
"I'll have a toasted ham and cheese sandwich and a large caesar salad please."
"Sure," she smiles and says, "coming right up."
The boys finish up their main course and outcomes Gary.
"Hi guys how are ya's?"
"Great Gary, and you?"
"Doing good, thank you!"
"All psyched for the playoffs?"
"You know it," replies David.
Tamara rounded the corner with two of her and Gary's friends.
"Hi David, Hi Stephen."
"Well hello there," they smile and say!!
"Thought ya's would have supper out after the big game ay?"
"Yep and why not, it's a Saturday," Stephen smiles and says.
"Guys I'd like you to meet Crystal."
David stands up and extends his hand."
"Hi Crystal, it's nice to meet you." Then Stephen does the same.
"It's a pleasure to meet you guys!" Crystal smiles and says.
"Movie time for us," Crystal smiles and says.
Gary, Tamara and Crystal start for the door.
"I'll be right with ya's guys," Larry smiles and says.
"Mr. Nicols are ya on a date?" asks Stephen. Larry smiles and says, "yep this is our seventh one. So we thought we would double date with Gary and Tamara."
"Well that's good!! Good for you, Mr. Nicols!" Stephen smiles and says.
"She seems very nice," replies David.
"Thanks," Larry smiles and says.
"She is a friend and co-worker of Tamara's and wanna know the best part guys?"

"Sure," David smiles and says.
"She is a Christian like us!"
"Good for you!! Good for you!!" David smiles and says.
"Well I gotta put myself back out there!!"
"That's excellent Mr. Nicols," Stephen replies.
"I wish you the best."
"Thanks!!"
"I better boogie!"
"Later guys!"
"Have fun tonight," says David. "Bye, bye."

Larry rushes out the door.
"That's just great," Stephen smiles and says.
"It sure is buddy, I'm happy for them!" replies David.
"Any dessert guys?" Stephen says, "I'll have a coffee, cream, sugar and a piece of lemon meringue pie. Me to please but no coffee for me thank you!!"Says david.
"Ok guys here ya go!"
"Thank you," replies David.
"One check this evening or two?"
"Just one please," says David.
The play offs are purely electric and the Leafs stay alive to the Stanley cup final!! Games six and seven were allotted to Toronto at home if needed. The 1990 final was between the Maple Leafs and Minnesota, North stars. Minnesota won the first game at home with a five to four win over the leafs. The second game Toronto won in a two period overtime play. Three to two. The third game at home they won by a two to zero shut out. At home the fourth game the Leafs pulled an amazing win on the road by clobbering the North Stars eight to two. It looked like the cup was right there for their taking. But I guess it really is true what they say, desperate times to call for desperate measures. In Minnesota Toronto didn't lack energy, intensity, skill drive or ambition. But neither did the North Stars and they had more of it. They pulled off a four to two win over the leafs.

"Good evening everyone on this beautiful late spring Thursday evening in Toronto. It's June 5th at 6:30 pm in a half an hour the puck is gonna drop. 1990 Stanley cup championship series Minnesota North stars versus the Toronto Maple leafs live at Maple Leaf Gardens. It's hockey night in Canada on CBC."
"Hello everyone I'm Andrew Sullivan with me as always Bob Thompson!"
"Hello everyone."
"Good evening Bob."
"Good evening Andrew, good evening everyone are ya ready for some great hockey tonight?"
"Bob absolutely a lot of us thought that the Leafs may pull off that Stanley cup victory on the road Tuesday night but Minnesota isn't gonna go down without a fight. Both teams Andrew had a great year."
"For sure Bob! Tyler Towes from Minnesota led the whole league this year in overtime goals. Brian Bosin was third in the league for assists. So the Leafs are definitely up against some stiff competition. Two minute commercial break when we return, Wendal Clark and David Gallagher will be joining us. You're watching Hockey Night in Canada on CBC."
"And we're back being joined now by Wendal Clark and David Gallagher guys thanks so much for talking with us for a few moments before the game."
"You're welcome Bob," replies Wendal and David. "Wendal what are your feelings going into game six tonight we have to be careful we have to be on guard look for the quick rebound."
"Absolutely," says Andrew.
"Do you think we were robbed, but home ice advantage probably played into it some I think?. One thing I've noticed all playoff season the North Stars have had a great defense. You score, you get past them and their goalie, you've earned it!"
"Wendal thank you so much for talking with us!"
"You're welcome."

"David how are you doing tonight?" "I'm great, thank you Bob, how are you?"

"I'm great, thanks." "So what do you think you and the rest of the Leafs can pull off a win tonight and stop the twenty three year Stanley cup drought to Toronto?"
"We're sure gonna try, Bob."
"What are your thoughts going into it?"
"I think Wendal was right when he brought up the rebounds. They gotta be hard and fast. I think they're passing techniques are very very fast as well. Gotta try to watch and study out what their next move will be. And I think try to be in the area they don't want us to be beforehand."
"David best of luck tonight."
"Thanks, Andrew.""You're no stranger to looking ahead at the strategic type of hockey are you?"
"No hard and fast hockey or brutish style hockey is popular but if we are gonna pull off a win tonight we gotta be hard and fast but also think strategically."
"I understand you and Stephen have a few special guests in the Gardens tonight."
"Yes, our pastor and his wife and Stephen's mom and dad are in the stands tonight and my mom and dad and two brothers and sister are all here tonight."
"That's great," says Andrew.
"Thank you, tonight I'm gonna do my best! I'd like to dedicate my playing tonight to my dad. As most of you know we thought we might lose him a couple years back. He had brain cancer but he is still with us. God totally healed him. And I'm so happy and proud to have him here tonight."
"That's great," replies Andrew.
"We wish you the best of luck tonight."
"Thanks Bob."
"Any final thoughts?"
"Yes, just one, It's a personal message to a good friend back home who I know is watching. LeRoy make plans for the shindig cause if I have my way. The cup and I will be making a trip home this summer!"
"Well alright, thank you David!"
"Thank you Wendal."

Miracle From First Pit Pond

National Anthems and puck drop when we return. Hockey night in Canada Stanley Cup Final game number six CBC."
Well at 9:39 pm David's wish came true. 9:39pm Toronto time on June 3rd, 1990. The official Stanley cup drought to the Toronto Maples Leafs was over. It was a magical night. David got an assist the first period and he scored the tying goal in period one and he scored the tying goal in period number two. In period number three the North Stars and leafs were tied three to three and with three minutes and four seconds remaining Todd Petten scored the winning goal!! The goal that led the Maple Leafs to Stanley Cup victory. Three minutes and four seconds, kinda iconic. David's jersey number was thirty four. Maybe Don Cherry was right, maybe Todd Petten, scrappy Stephen Theriault and David Gallagher were Toronto's new dream team!!
I tend to think Don was probably right. Stephen accepted another two year offer from the Leafs and Todd played with the leafs his entire nine year NHL career and in 1992 Todd, Stephen, and David won the Maple Leafs another Stanley Cup! They won it on the road against Calgary in seven games.

David Michael Gallagher played NHL hockey for thirteen years. He retired from playing on May 7th that year when his team the St. Louis Blues got beat out in the semi final by the Calgary Flames. David enjoyed a long thirteen year NHL career. His first six years he played for the Toronto Maple Leafs his seventh and eighth years he played for the Vancouver Canucks. For his 9th, 10th, 11th, 12th year he played for the Los Angeles Kings. And his 13th and final year, he played for the St. Louis Blues. David enjoyed three Stanley Cup victories in his career. Two with Toronto and one with Los Angeles. David enjoyed two years as assistant captain with the Los Angeles Kings.

Scrappy Stephen Theriault enjoyed a long seventeen year career in the NHL he enjoyed four Stanley cup victories. The first seven years of his career he was with the Toronto Maple Leafs. Where he enjoyed two Stanley Cup Victories. His 8th, 9th, 10th, 11th, 12th he was with the Chicago Black Hawks where he enjoyed a third Stanley Cup Victory, 13th, 14th with the Boston Bruins. And the

15th, 16th, 17th years with the Pittsburgh Penguins where he enjoyed his fourth and final Stanley Cup victory. Chris Chellios and Luc Robatie both said that Stephen Theriault was one of the nicest, kindest, meekest people they ever had the pleasure of playing hockey against. But the name always stuck with Stephen Scrappy Stephen Theriault because of the incident in his NHL rookie year in his first regular season game!!
Ha, ha, ha, ha nobody messes with scrappy Stephen Theriault's crease. LeRoy Garnder kept his word. Gerry McNamara and scrappy Stephen and David and all the First Pit Pond miracles and about two hundred and seventeen people from St. Croix, New Brunswick and other surrounding communities got to see Lord Stanley's cup and have some fine steak and lobster and scallops the Bay of Fundy and New Brunswick can produce. Oh and the beef comes from? Where else? The Gallagher family farm. James Chapter 5: 15-16 from the Bible came true for Micaeal Gallagher he never ever was sick with cancer again. He passed away at the age of sixty-two of a heart attack. But not before he enjoyed three years of retirement and five grandchildren to his credit.

Larry Nicols and Crystal got married and enjoyed a long happy life. Every summer they take a little vacation down east and they always spend a day or two visiting Sarah.

Donna June Gallagher lived to be a ripe old age of eighty three years old. In her life she raised four great kids. She enjoyed eight grandchildren and one great grandchild and a wonderful second husband for the last nine year of her life. Joseph worked on the family farm for his mom and dad till it got sold in 2005. He got married and enjoyed his children, two girls and a boy for Joseph.

Kevin Gallagher enjoyed building things and he took a course in carpentry and renovations. He married a wonderful lady who was a nurse. They enjoyed a son and daughter. Remember earlier we learned that Joseph worked for his mom and dad until the family farm sold in 2005. Joseph went to work for the new owner and has worked there ever since.

In 2005 Sarah Elizabeth Gallagher bought the family farm from her mom and dad. She has expanded it. Sarah has over nine employees including her brother Joseph. Sarah Elizabeth fell in love and got married. She and her husband enjoy two beautiful little identical twin daughters. Who are the spitting image of their mom!! And off the record they always seem to have their mama's spunk and drive to!! And every year they always look forward to going to uncle David's for three weeks every summer. In Seabrook, New Hampshire.

David Michael Gallagher spends his days now as assistant coach for the Boston Bruins. Every year he drives six and a half hours home to St. Croix, New Brunswick for three weeks holiday then back to Seabrook with his nieces. Then three weeks later back home to St. Croix, New Brunswick to take the girls back to their home on the family farm. David has a wife and a little boy named Michael Stephen Gallagher who he named in honour of his dad and best friend! And just think none of this may have been possible. May have never happened had it not been for a miracle. The miracle from First Pit Pond.

Frederick Demerchant